The
Empty
Nest
Chronicles

The Empty Nest Chronicles

HOW TO HAVE FUN
(AND STOP ANNOYING YOUR SPOUSE)
AFTER THE KIDS MOVE OUT

JERRY ZEZIMA

*Nationally syndicated humorist and author of
"Leave It to Boomer"*

iUniverse LLC
Bloomington

THE EMPTY NEST CHRONICLES
How to Have Fun (and Stop Annoying Your Spouse) After the Kids Move Out

iUniverse books may be ordered through booksellers or by contacting:

iUniverse LLC
1663 Liberty Drive
Bloomington, IN 47403
www.iuniverse.com
1-800-Authors (1-800-288-4677)

ISBN: 978-1-4917-0165-2 (sc)
ISBN: 978-1-4917-0166-9 (ebk)

Printed in the United States of America

iUniverse rev. date: 08/07/2013

Contents

Dedication

For my mother, Rosina, and in memory of my father, Jerry, Sr., the family's original empty nesters, this book is dedicated with love and gratitude.

Acknowledgments

To my wife, Sue, to whom I have been married for thirty-five wonderful years, thanks for all of your love and for happily sharing the nest with a birdbrain.

To our daughters, Katie and Lauren, who may have left the nest but are always in our hearts, thanks for filling our home with love and laughter, not to mention a lot of stuff that really needs to be cleaned out.

To my sons-in-law, Dave and Guillaume, thanks for loving my daughters, for being such great guys, and for laughing at my jokes when all the women in the family just roll their eyes.

To our great friends and fellow empty nesters, the Lovelettes and the Richerts, thanks for letting me tell your stories and for all the good times we have had. The next round is on me.

To John Breunig, the editor of my hometown paper, The Stamford Advocate in Connecticut, thanks for saving my humor column from extinction and for continuing to run it even though we both know that it has no redeeming social value. Ditto to former Advocate editor David McCumber, who blessedly doesn't have to deal with it anymore. To Dieter Stanko and Jon Lucas of The Advocate, thanks for kindly and cheerfully putting up with me. And to Erin Walsh of Hearst Connecticut Media Group, thanks for your delightful wit and for making sure I get paid.

To Karen Denny of the McClatchy-Tribune News Service, thanks for distributing my column to papers across the country and for failing to realize that I am the reason journalism is in trouble.

To Arianna Huffington, thanks for making me a regular contributor to the Huffington Post. I can only assume that you're not really sure who I am.

To Rob Fouch, ace editor and budding novelist, thanks for your helpful suggestions, none of which involved burning the manuscript.

To Ronnie Gill, crackerjack journalist and computer wizard, thanks for helping me overcome my technological incompetence to get this book to the publisher.

To Debby Krenek, Debbie Henley, Rich Rosen, and Jack Millrod, thanks for risking the franchise to get my column on Newsday.com. I'm surprised the site hasn't crashed yet.

To my agent, Janet Rosen, of Sheree Bykofsky Associates, thanks for your hard work, good humor, and continued support, all of which have resulted in this book. I hope the literary establishment will forgive you.

To Kim West, Barry Lee, Cherry Noel, and the rest of the team at iUniverse, thanks for helping to make this book, my second for the publishing house, a reality. You were very brave to have taken on such a dubious project.

To anyone else who helped me, thanks for helping me. I'm sorry your names escape me at the moment, but at this age, these things happen.

Introduction

This is the story of two people who live in an empty nest.
One of them has an empty head. The other one
loves him anyway.

Sue and I met in high school, Stamford Catholic, Class of 1971, in our hometown of Stamford, Connecticut. I can't say I grew up there because, as you will soon see, I haven't grown up.

Then we went to Saint Michael's College in Colchester, Vermont, and graduated in the Class of 1975, Sue with a BA in English, I with a BS in life.

We weren't high school sweethearts or even college sweethearts because we didn't date steadily in either high school or college, but I knew Sue was a sweetheart because she was, of course, sweet, as well as smart, petite, and beautiful, all in one irresistible package. I fell head over heels. It took a week for the swelling to go down.

Three years after college, we were married. Two years after that, we were parents.

Katie came into the world on July 17, 1980. Lauren followed on November 13, 1982. By kindergarten, they were more mature than I was.

When the girls were still in elementary school, we moved from a small apartment in Stamford to a condominium that was twenty-three feet from the back door of our old place. It would have been easier to pack up and move to California.

Nine years later, we did pack up and move again, this time to a nice house on Long Island, New York. In three months, Katie was off to college. In two years, so was Lauren.

They were both gone. And the nest was empty.

It happened because Sue and I blinked. If only we had kept our eyes open, the girls wouldn't have grown up so fast and would still be living at home.

Now the house is so quiet you can hear a pin drop. Of course, it's never a good idea to drop a pin in the house because you won't find it for days. Then it will turn up in the bottom of your foot, which will bleed all over the carpet and perhaps become infected, necessitating either surgery or amputation. It's a pretty steep price to pay just to prove a point, which is that the house can get eerily silent after your kids move out.

That is what Sue and I found out after Katie and Lauren left the nest. This isn't to say that there is never any noise in our humble abode. Sometimes it's filled with the sound of snoring, which comes from one or both of us as we sit in front of the television on a typically action-packed weekday night and struggle to stay awake for the eleven o'clock news.

Let's just say that life is different when you're an empty nester. All those years of play dates (before the kids became too embarrassed to be seen with you) and ringing telephones (they were never for you) and requests to borrow the car (if your children would be kind enough to give you the keys) are over.

These are the times that try men's souls. And their marriages. Same goes for wives, who realize, now that the kids are gone, just how annoying their husbands really are.

But this also can be a great time of life, a chance for couples to rediscover each other. Sure, you miss your kids, but they'll be back, most likely to mooch a meal or drop off stuff they want you to store for them.

That's the way Sue and I look at it. This book is a record of our lives since the girls moved out. All of the people are real and all of the stories are true. Any embellishment is the result of too much beer.

That reminds me: Sue and I have a date Saturday night at our favorite burger joint. Where else would an empty nester take his sweetheart?

Chapter 1

You're on your own, parents. After all those years of a full house, the nest is now empty. But the kids always leave a little bit of themselves (correction: a lot of it) behind. Here's how it happened in our humble home.

"A Moving Experience"

Katie and Lauren aren't living at home anymore and it's all my fault. That's because, like many empty nesters, I am a mover and shaker: When the kids left the nest, I had to do most of the moving, after which I started shaking.

It all began when Katie went to college in Boston. Until then, the heaviest lifting I did was helping Sue with the groceries. Now I was expected to lug furniture, boxes, and suitcases that felt like they contained anvils, or at least dead bodies, up and down stairs so they could be placed in, then taken out of, dorm rooms that would soon be messy enough to be condemned by the board of health.

My health, which had been excellent, because I avoided all forms of exercise for the simple reason that they could kill me, began its rapid decline after these Olympic weightlifting events.

I was already a veteran of four years of college moving, and was facing two more until Lauren got out, when Katie announced that she wasn't coming back home. She had fallen in love with Boston and decided to stay there. This meant all the stuff from her dormitory had to be moved into her new apartment, the downstairs half of an old but charming two-story house in a hilly neighborhood near the city line. Before that could happen, however, I had to rent a truck that turned out to be in even worse shape than I was and load it with stuff from our house on Long Island—including our beloved old couch. Then I had to drive up to Boston, park the truck outside

Katie's new digs, attend graduation, go back to her apartment, and begin carting things in while praying that I didn't suffer an attack of apoplexy or rupture a vital organ.

The truck adventure will go down in my increasingly fading memory as the Trip From Hell. I say this for two reasons: (a) the truck was in such horrible condition that if it were a person, it would have been given last rites, and (b) I had to drive this pathetic heap, which wheezed and bucked and leaked fluids, much as I do when I get out bed in the morning, through a rainstorm of, fittingly, biblical proportions. God only knows how I made it.

But make it I did. Like a man possessed, I embarked on the torturous process of moving Katie in. The torture was eased somewhat with several lifesaving infusions of cold beer.

The next day, I drove home with Sue to a nest that was half-empty. That's because Lauren was still there. Two years later, she got out of college, which she attended in Connecticut, and lived at home for a while before fulfilling a promise she made at approximately age nine of someday getting a place of her own.

On moving day, I had to rent another truck. This one, while in better shape than the one I got to move Katie, was nonetheless the same model year as the Flintstones' car and couldn't have reached the speed limit if it had plummeted off a cliff.

Outside of the truck, on the overhang above the driver's-side door, was this sign: "WARNING: Watch your head before entering or exiting the cab." I did so before entering the cab, but because the sign wasn't on the inside of the truck, and because I couldn't have watched my head unless I looked in the mirror, I forgot all about it when exiting the cab.

After pulling into the parking lot outside Lauren's apartment, I got out, stood up, heard a sickening thud, felt a sudden bolt of pain on the top of my head, and realized that I not only may have given myself a concussion but also may have dented the truck to the extent that I'd probably be charged extra when I returned it. Fortunately, neither the truck nor my head suffered permanent damage.

The rest of the day was spent moving Lauren in. I must say that her apartment was cute and was in a nice complex in a good neighborhood. I must also say that Sue and I missed her, just as we

2

missed Katie. Now the emptiness of the nest was complete because both girls were gone.

This did not mean, however, that my moving days were over. A year later, after her lease was up, Lauren moved again because one of her neighbors, a real creep, had given her so much trouble that she decided to transfer to another apartment in the complex. Her new place was not far enough away to have justified renting a truck, which would have made moving the heavy stuff easier, but it wasn't close enough to have significantly cut down the number of steps Sue and I had to take while hauling all of Lauren's worldly possessions.

We stuffed a lot of stuff, which is why it's called stuff, into the back of my SUV and drove it diagonally across the parking lot, from Apartment 66 to Apartment 12, where we unstuffed it and, speaking of steps, carried it upstairs.

I forgot to mention, possibly because of a ruptured blood vessel in my head, that Lauren's old apartment was on the first floor and that her new apartment was on the second floor. This added the maximum amount of exertion to the move. I wouldn't have expected anything less.

What Sue and I couldn't cram into my car, we carried, slowly and awkwardly, across the parking lot and up the stairs of Lauren's new place. Once, while lugging a huge box containing cups, saucers, and plates, I tripped on the steps and banged my knee. It began to bleed. At least I didn't fall down the stairs and break my neck.

While carrying a bedspring with Sue, I also sliced my finger. The only thing that held it on was one of Lauren's Hello Kitty Band-Aids. Sue suffered her share of scrapes and bruises, too. Fortunately, we had help from Mike and Heather, who lived next to the jerk who was bothering Lauren, and from Lauren's friend Stephanie and her boyfriend, also named Mike. Lauren pitched in, too, although mostly she supervised. She was very good at it.

It took ten hours, from one in the afternoon until eleven at night, to move Lauren in, but it was well worth it because her new apartment was bigger and nicer than her old one. It also overlooked the water.

"This is beautiful," I said on many pleasant visits as Sue and I sat on Lauren's small deck, sipping cocktails and watching the boats go by. I also said (to myself), "Thank God, I'll never have to move her again."

That's what I thought. Over the next two years, the company that owned the complex proved so pathetically incompetent—the billing department lost several of Lauren's rent payments, the maintenance guys couldn't fix a leak that damaged the ceiling and walls of the apartment, the same bozos locked Lauren's dog outside on the deck in the broiling heat after they supposedly finished another failed repair job—that I was convinced it was run by Congress.

So was Lauren. Which is why she found yet another apartment, this one about five miles away. I will spare you the painful details of the move, but they involved carrying bulky and dangerously weighty furniture up a narrow stairwell and, even worse, putting together a butcher's block, a job that took an entire afternoon because it was done by a butcher's blockhead.

Soon thereafter, Lauren met Guillaume. Shortly after that, they decided to move in together. As the father of a young woman, I was naturally concerned about the situation and expressed my apprehension to Sue when I said, "Oh, no! Not another move!"

Guillaume, about whom I had no concerns because I quickly realized he was a wonderful young man, proved it by smartly hiring professional movers.

"He's a good boy," Sue said. I agreed.

We felt the same way about Dave, who had moved in with Katie not long after she got her apartment in Boston. They were married a couple of years later.

After living in the apartment for several years, they announced that they were moving to Michigan.

"Here we go again," I thought. But Dave, like Guillaume, hired professional movers.

The only item I had to deal with was the couch Sue and I gave to Katie when she graduated from college. This couch had great sentimental value because it was our first major piece of furniture, a brown, beige, and gold work of upholstered craftsmanship dating back to 1978, when Sue and I got married.

The couch was also called the sofa because I'd relax on it while I should have been doing household chores and would say to Sue,

"Sofa, so good," to which she would reply, "Maybe you'd like to sleep on it tonight."

It was almost as comfortable as our bed, though with slightly less legroom. It also was durable enough to withstand the worst kind of abuse, such as spills (beer, soda, baby formula) and soils (from Katie and Lauren before they were potty trained). The messes were easily wiped away because the couch was made of some super-resistant, possibly bulletproof material that did not, unfortunately, repel cat and dog hair.

The couch was a repository for food—pretzels, popcorn, and potato chips—that had been dropped between the cushions. A yearly cleaning could have produced enough nourishment to feed Luxembourg.

I often munched away on the couch because it was my ringside seat for televised sporting events. I parked myself there for Super Bowl clashes, World Series showdowns, Stanley Cup contests, and March Madness matchups. When a big game wasn't on, I would watch something intellectual, like the Three Stooges.

The couch will go down in posterity, if not prosperity, as the site of an infamous photo taken one Halloween when I dressed up as Groucho Marx and our next-door neighbor, Frank, dressed up as a lady of the evening, complete with a wig, lipstick, stockings, and a padded dress. I must say, he looked pretty good. We sat next to each other on the couch as Sue took our picture. If it ever turns up, I could lose thousands of dollars in blackmail money.

The best couch photo of all time did turn up when Dave found an old shot of the girls that Katie had stashed away. He posted it on Facebook. Katie, who was about three years old, was sitting on the couch with two Strawberry Shortcake dolls and a box of Cheerios; Lauren, who was one, was leaning against the couch, sucking her thumb. Under the photo was the announcement that the couch was for sale. But there were no takers.

Sue and I spent the weekend with Katie and Dave as they prepared to move. For two nights, Sue slept on the couch. "I had two of the best nights' sleep of my life on that dumb thing," she said.

That morning, Dave and I carried it to the curb, where it was claimed by the garbageman. Maybe he took it home, but more likely it went to the dump and was crushed to kindling.

Farewell, old couch. Rest in pieces.

"The Wrong Stuff"

I had always thought that my garage was the stuff of legend because it's stuffed with stuff, most of which isn't my stuff but my daughters' stuff. It has been accumulating since they left the nest, which supposedly is empty because they don't live at home anymore but really isn't because a lot of their stuff is still here.

Then I talked with my college buddy and longtime friend Tim Lovelette, who not only has a garage full of his kids' stuff but a basement full of it, too, which makes both places the stuff of legend.

"If our kids' stuff had any value, they wouldn't trust us with it. They'd be using it," Tim told me. "Why have we got it? Because they don't want it. This is nefarious, no question about it. Somehow, a whole generation has gotten together and conspired to fill our homes with worthless stuff."

Tim has more stuff than I do because he and his wife, Jane, have three adult children, Marshall, Amy, and Brendan, while Sue and I have Katie and Lauren. They're all great kids, even though they aren't, technically, kids anymore. Still, when you get to be my age (old enough to know better), practically everyone else is a kid. So here's looking at you, kids. And all your stuff.

"I think somebody's got a key to the house and brings stuff in," Tim theorized. "I change the locks and it still goes on."

This means the reverse robber is leaving stuff not only in Tim's garage but in his basement, a problem I don't have because I don't have a basement.

"You're not qualified to have adult children if you don't have a basement," Tim said. "Where are they going to put their stuff?"

"In the garage," I replied.

"You wouldn't appreciate anything until you've seen my garage," Tim said. "How many bicycles can you accumulate in a lifetime? I don't even like bicycles."

Another thing Tim has in his garage is the snow blower he bought for Marshall.

"I bought it for him for Christmas three or four years ago," Tim recalled, adding that Marshall's wife, Sara, said she would buy Marshall a shed for his birthday so he could put the snow blower in it. "But she never bought the shed," Tim said. "Now I have two snow blowers in my garage. Sara and Marshall have a basement, but there can't be anything in it, including the snow blower. I don't think it's ever been started, but it's there, ready to go, in my garage."

Then there are all those skis and ice skates.

"How many pairs of skis can you accumulate?" Tim wondered. "Just go to my garage and count them and figure it out. And I have all their ice skates. My kids haven't ice-skated in fifteen years. If they had to use this stuff, which is all out of date, they'd go out and buy new ones and leave the old ones in my house."

"What about the basement?" I asked.

"You wouldn't believe it," Tim replied. "It's filled with He-Man toys. You wouldn't know about them because you have girls, but these toys go back twenty or thirty years. This whole thing must go back to prehistoric times. I can envision caves, with Neanderthal-type people, caves filled with stuff, and the kids are saying, 'No, you can't throw away my bones.' It's been going on for centuries."

"What can we do about it?" I said.

"Pack up their stuff in a moving van and have it delivered to them," Tim answered. "Or have a yard sale. If you have ever gone to a yard sale, you'd see that there's always a free table. All the stuff you have that belongs to your kids should go on the free table. Just tell them, 'I'm giving your stuff away.' What can they do? They can't hit us."

"Then we'd have the last laugh," I said.

"Not really," said Tim. "There's a final resolution to all of this: When we die, our kids will have a houseful of stuff—not just their stuff but our stuff. They'll say, 'What are we going to do with Dad's stuff?' Answer: They'll have a yard sale. Our stuff will go on the free table."

7

I didn't want the situation to get to that point. That's why I liked Tim's idea of a pre-emptive strike. So I had a yard sale. Or, as such an event is called on Long Island, a tag sale.

To run a tag sale, you need two things: stuff and Bloody Marys. We had a lot more stuff than we had Bloody Marys, but the Bloody Marys went faster than the stuff.

Joining us in this disastrous venture was Lauren.

Among the items we put out in the driveway and on the front lawn were: two pairs of crutches ($5 and $10), the Bubble Mate Foot Bubbler ($10), a wok ($5), a dog cage ($20), a pair of ice skates ($5), two artificial Christmas trees ($10 and $20), and a painting of two barns in a field ($15), plus lots of clothes (reasonably priced) and costume jewelry (ditto).

The sale began at ten a.m. Sue, Lauren, and I sat on chairs in the driveway with a cash box (empty) and glasses of Bloody Marys (full), ready to do a brisk business.

At eleven a.m., a guy named Marty came by.

"Times must be tough if you're having a tag sale," he said.

"Not at all," I replied. "I'm dependently wealthy."

"What do you mean?" Marty asked.

"I'm depending on you to make me wealthy," I said.

Marty left without buying anything.

"You're driving customers away," Sue told me.

"We'll have to sell you," Lauren chimed in.

"And take a loss," Sue said.

"Who loses money at their own tag sale?" Lauren wondered.

"We do," Sue noted.

"It's pathetic," said Lauren, adding, "Who wants another Bloody Mary?"

At eleven-thirty, we made our first sale. A woman named Rosa admired the watercolor of the barns.

"I painted it myself," I said.

"Really?" Rosa chirped.

"No," I admitted.

"Ten dollars," she offered. It was five bucks less than the price on the tag. I drive a hard bargain, so I said, "Sold!"

A man named J.R. drove up with his children, Ana, five, and James, three, who wanted Lauren's art set. I played hide-and-seek with the kids as J.R. handed Lauren $10, which she put in the cash box.

"Bye, Jerry!" the kids shouted from the car as J.R. drove away.

A woman who stopped with her adult daughter told us that she had recently been in a car accident.

"If you get into another one," I said helpfully, "we have crutches." No sale.

A young guy showed up to look at the jewelry.

"I made it when I was in prison," I told him.

"You did a nice job," he said.

"I had a lot of time," I replied.

"Prisoners generally do," said the guy, who bought $12 worth of rings and earrings for his wife.

By three p.m., the official end of the sale, $55 sat in the cash box. We lugged most of the unsold stuff back into the garage and sent out for dinner, which came to $67.

"Next time we have a tag sale," Lauren said, "we should give Bloody Marys to the customers. Maybe then we'll make a profit."

Chapter 2

All empty nesters need other empty nesters to commiserate with. For Sue and me, it's our longtime friends Tim and Jane Lovelette and Hank and Angela Richert.

"The Lovelettes"

I met Tim in college. He lived in the next dorm room. On the first day of our freshman year, Tim surreptitiously introduced himself by waiting until my roommate, Hank Richert, and I went to dinner. Then Tim and his roommate, Peter Keefe, took all the furniture out of our room. If that weren't enough, Tim brought up a dog he found in the quad and put the pooch in the empty room. She was later released, happy and unharmed, but the episode clued me in to Tim's unique brand of prankishness. It also was the beginning of a beautiful friendship.

Tim and I have been kindred spirits—and have shared many spirits—ever since.

One of the things we have in common—aside from a pathological compulsion to play practical jokes, make stupid remarks to complete strangers, and otherwise act like overgrown, immature idiots, much to the chagrin of our wives—is that we are now empty nesters.

That Tim's kids have grown up to be wonderful young people is due in large part to Tim, both because of and in spite of his predilection for the aforementioned behavior. But it's due in even larger part to Jane, whom he met in first grade and began dating in high school.

Tim and Jane were married in junior year of college and moved into an apartment in Winooski, Vermont. This meant Tim wasn't living on campus anymore. Things were a lot quieter in the dorm, but at least Hank and I no longer had to worry about missing furniture or errant dogs.

After graduation, Tim and Jane moved back to Cape Cod, Massachusetts, where they grew up, and started raising a family. Sue and I were simultaneously raising our family in Stamford. We and the girls often spent our summer vacations on the Cape with the Lovelettes.

At breakfast during one of our early visits, I was sitting at the kitchen table with a plate full of eggs and bacon that Jane had made when I turned around to reach for the orange juice. When I turned back around to my plate, the bacon was gone.

I couldn't identify the culprit because all five kids were giggling loudly and holding up their hands to show it wasn't them. Since Amy was sitting next to me, I pinned the rap on her. She grinned widely—with a mouthful of food—and shook her head in innocence. Jane gave me more bacon, and when I turned around again, it was gone.

Bacon pilfering has been part of the routine ever since. No matter where we have been—in Tim and Jane's kitchen, a diner, or a hotel restaurant—one of the Lovelette kids has stolen my bacon. At least they've helped me cut down on my cholesterol.

The years flew by and the kids grew up, something they tend to do, especially when you feed them. Before we knew it, one by one, they went off to college. Then, inevitably, they started getting married.

The first to tie the knot was Marshall, who married Sara in a quaint New England church on a crisp day just after Christmas. It was the first time anyone in my circle of friends (who can barely form a circle, especially after a couple of beers) had a child who was getting married.

Sue and I arrived at the church with Katie and Lauren. We greeted Jane, who looked beautiful, and Tim, who looked almost respectable. Jane beamed with happiness and excitement as she embraced each of us. Tim smiled, too, but he seemed a little nervous.

"It's hot in here," he said as he fiddled with his collar.

It wasn't hot at all. I knew I had to say something to put him at ease, to calm him on this joyous occasion with words that would be fitting and proper for a blessed time in a solemn setting.

"Your fly is open," I said.

Tim looked down, saw that it wasn't, laughed heartily, threw his arms around me, and said, "You big goof!"

The ceremony was simple and lovely. Sara and Marshall were a luminous couple. As the wedding party walked out of church, I watched as Tim and Jane, and Sara's parents, Ted and Ellie, strolled happily by. I looked at Sue. She looked at me. We both looked over at Katie and Lauren, who were chatting about something that no doubt involved what they were going to order from the bar at the reception.

When your children selfishly insist on eating every day, then have the gall to go to college, and one day get married, money becomes a precious commodity. The only thing that ran through my mind was: "To pay for their weddings, I'll have to rob a bank." Then I corrected myself: "Two banks."

As we moved on to the receiving line, I couldn't help but notice that Tim seemed greatly relieved.

"You made it," I said.

"It's a miracle," he replied. "And I didn't fall on my face."

I said, "Wait until the reception."

Tim didn't fall on his face there, either, because he and Jane had taken dancing lessons to prepare themselves for the big day.

One of the highlights of the reception was when Ted, the father of the bride, made a toast in which he said he was moved to tears because (pausing for effect), "The wedding cake has tiers."

Everybody groaned.

I thought: "One day, that will be me." I also thought: "I have to remember that line."

All in all, it was a wonderful day, filled with love and laughter and the joy of seeing old friends so happy.

The happiness continued almost three years later, when Katie and Dave got married, which made me the first guy in our circle of friends to be father of the bride. Naturally, all the Lovelettes were at the wedding. My toast, which would have made Spencer Tracy and Steve Martin proud, lasted about as long as a State of the Union address. Unfortunately, I forgot Ted's line about tears.

The following year, Tim and Jane became the first people in that same circle to become grandparents. That's when Anna, Sara and Marshall's beautiful daughter, was born.

When Anna was five months old, Sue and I went up to the Cape for a visit, during which we met not only Anna but a great guy named Mel, Amy's fiance. This meant Tim would be following in my large and stumbling footsteps as father of the bride.

As we sat back for a meeting of the minds (or what passed for them, since cocktails were involved), Tim reminisced fondly about the moment when he found out he was a grandfather. "I demanded a paternity test for Marshall," he said. "I'm still not a grandfather. In the absence of the test, I'm not sure the whole thing is going to stick."

According to an official source (Jane), it did, so Tim picked the name he wanted Anna to call him when she learned to talk. His choice: Big Daddy. "Not for any other reason than that Jane will have to be known as Big Mama," said Tim, who acknowledged that he had to lose a few pounds for Amy and Mel's wedding. Jane, a marathon runner, is anything but big, so eventually Anna started calling her Go-Go.

Then the subject of changing diapers came up. Would Tim do it? "Not at all," he said firmly. "I'm world-famous for not performing my fatherly duties, so it's advancing one generation."

What about bottle feeding? "I'll bring a quart of liquor and a nipple," Tim said. "I'll outdrink the baby."

And what words of wisdom did Tim give to Marshall? "Hide. Get out of the house. Pretend you have to go to work. Your qualities as a father will be pretty limited, so take up fishing, boating, get a second job if you have to."

Speaking of jobs, Marshall works for Tim at Marshall K. Lovelette Insurance, a third-generation agency on the Cape that was founded by Tim's father. When Marshall brought Anna to the office for the first time, recalled Tim, "Every woman in the place had to hold her. There was zero production. It set business back three years in one trip. She's the most expensive baby ever born."

Tim, of course, said all of this with tongue in cheek, which made him pretty hard to understand. He was thrilled to be a grandfather, which was obvious when Sue and I met Anna, without question the best-behaved baby in the world. She developed a regular sleeping pattern her second night home.

"That first night was tough," Marshall acknowledged. "I've been recovering ever since."

Also, Anna didn't scream or cry when she saw me. In fact, she cooed and laughed and let me hold her while Marshall snapped a picture of us. After Anna went to bed, I had a few words of advice for Tim about his upcoming duties as father of the bride.

"Your chief role," I informed him, "is to be like a bobblehead doll: Just keep nodding. And sign everything that is put in front of you. Otherwise, stay the hell out of the way."

"I've already done my part," Tim said. "I've agreed to show up."

And show up Tim did—along with Jane, of course—to Amy and Mel's wedding, which was fabulous. Tim, who did indeed shed those extra pounds, gave a moving toast that neither lasted as long as mine at Katie and Dave's wedding nor included Ted's tears line at Sara and Marshall's.

The following morning, at breakfast in the hotel restaurant, just before she and Mel left for their honeymoon, Amy stole my bacon.

Not long afterward, Brendan moved out of the house to live with his girlfriend. It was official: Tim and Jane were empty nesters. Finally, like Sue and me, they had time to spend with each other. And, lo, there was a revelation.

"All those years, as Jane was raising the children and I was doing my own thing at the office, what was really happening was that I was becoming fantastically annoying," Tim acknowledged. "She didn't know it, but now that we have this time together, there isn't a thing I do that doesn't annoy the poor woman. She had her back turned and I grew annoying. I didn't know I was that annoying, to be honest with you. Now that there's adequate communication, it's not a secret anymore."

When I told Jane what Tim said about how annoying he is and how she never realized it, she replied, "I've known that forever."

Still, it's love and laughter that have kept them together. Many years earlier, at a party on the Cape to celebrate their twenty-fifth wedding anniversary, Tim toasted Jane by saying, "She's the backbone of the family."

Like Sue, Jane is selfless in her devotion to her loved ones. But that doesn't mean she hasn't found time for herself.

"I took up running at forty-seven," said Jane, who has worked in the office at the family insurance business. "The kids were all leaving the house. I saw an ad in the paper for a women's walk-and-run fitness program. I joined. And I got hooked."

Jane has run in about twenty marathons, including about ten Boston Marathons. She has also run in Vermont, Philadelphia, Chicago, Las Vegas, and Niagara Falls.

"My fastest time was in Philly, where I finished fourth," Jane said. "My highest finish was third, in both Las Vegas and Niagara Falls. This is for women in my age group. They call us seniors, which is kind of rude."

Jane looks like anything but a senior. Like Sue, who does a lot of walking, she keeps in fantastic shape. But she also cherishes time with Tim.

"It's more relaxing now that the kids are out of the house," Jane said. "We see them plenty, but it's nice to have quiet time to yourself. You get to know each other again. There's more time to sit and relax with each other, even if we're not doing anything."

For Tim—still an incorrigible joker and a devoted family man who hasn't taken up running but loves to go fishing on his boat—Jane's words were nice to hear.

"My wife says I'm better than nothing," he noted. "I guess she's right."

"The Richerts"

I knew Hank even before I met Tim. Hank and I go all the way back to high school, where we both had a keen interest in two subjects: goofing off and girls. Neither of us was voted Most Likely to Succeed in the latter, but we did show great proficiency in the former. That we both married the girls of our dreams and are still goofing off is a testament to the excellent education we got at Catholic High.

Here is how Hank was described in our yearbook:

Henry J. Richert
Hank

A rifleman . . . enjoys bowling . . . always on the road in
that powerful VW . . . seems to be out for a good time . . .
never takes things too seriously . . . humorous . . . witty . . .
trustworthy.

I'm not sure about the rifleman part, unless you count the shots
he did in college, but Hank was an ace at the lanes, has never taken
things too seriously, and has always been out for a good time. He
is, indeed, humorous, witty, and trustworthy. And that powerful
VW, the front end of which is shown in our yearbook being lifted
in the snowy Stamford Catholic parking lot by Hank and five other
classmates, was replaced during our college years by an even more
powerful VW. Affectionately dubbed "Trusty Cruiser," it saved the
lives of Hank, Sue, and yours truly during a blizzard in Vermont on
a harrowing drive back to school.

In fact, it was college that reunited the three of us. I knew Sue
and Hank casually in high school. I liked Hank a lot. And, frankly,
I had the hots for Sue. So when I found out they were going to St.
Mike's, I decided to go there, too. Fortunately, the school lowered
its otherwise high standards to let me in. That the place survived
the notorious Class of 1975—which included me, Sue, Hank, and,
of course, Tim—and is now one of the top-rated small colleges in
America says a lot about its resilience as an institution.

One of the best things about going to Saint Michael's, for me,
was that Hank and I were roommates for three years. I majored
in political science, not because I was interested in politics, or
even science, but because Hank was a poli-sci major and I figured
he would know his way to class, which meant I could follow him
around campus and not get lost. I also figured that, since Hank was
intelligent and responsible, he would pay attention during lectures,
and if I missed something, or fell asleep, or didn't show up at all, he
would help me out. This worked pretty well until it came time to

take exams. For some reason, Hank always got better grades than I did.

We also did our share of partying. In our sophomore or junior year, Playboy rated St. Mike's as the third-biggest party school in either the East or the entire country, I forget which, probably because I was partying when I read it. Anyway, it was the first time in my life that I had a sense of accomplishment. Hank contributed, too. And since the drinking age in Vermont was eighteen at the time, Hank and I—beer lovers whose tastes, or lack thereof, tended toward products such as Schlitz—did our part to keep the American brewing industry solvent.

Of course, we had our share of adventures. One of the most memorable was a ski trip to Madonna Mountain, which was named not for the famous singer, who wasn't yet famous, but for the Mother of God, to whom pathetic skiers such as Hank and myself often prayed.

If you combined our talents, we were terrific. Separately, we were terrible. I didn't know how to snowplow, but I could stop on a dime. Hank was the opposite: He could snowplow, but he couldn't stop.

We arrived late in the morning and, without so much as a lesson, went up to the beginners' slope. On one of my runs down the hill, I saw the far-off figure of a man gliding into my path and then out of it, into it, then out of it. Since I couldn't do anything except go in a straight line, I worried that he would cut into my path at precisely the wrong moment.

Which is precisely what happened. I flattened the poor guy, who lay motionless in the snow. Almost immediately, I was face-to-face with a member of the ski patrol, who saw the whole thing and yelled, "Don't you know how to ski?" Naturally, I took great offense at this and replied, "No."

The man, who had literally been knocked out, rolled over. I saw that he was about eighty years old. He sat up, glared at me, and threatened to skewer me with one of his ski poles.

"Sorry," I said weakly. Then I whirled around and continued on my reckless run.

Meanwhile, Hank was slowly approaching the bottom of the hill. Realizing he couldn't stop, he flopped down on his belly and slid into a bunch of people who were taking a skiing lesson. He bowled most of them over, leaving the 7-10 split.

At this point, I came up with an idea that explains why I got a D in logic: I suggested to Hank that we try the intermediate slope because, as I reasoned, "There'll be fewer people to run into up there."

There weren't. To make a long story even longer, we had several more mishaps, including one in which I knocked a woman into the woods and another in which Hank and I ran into each other. It took us the rest of the day to get down the mountain. After that run, Hank and I—cold, wet, and tired—went to the lodge for some much-needed beer and a hot dinner. Then we went back to school and lapsed into comas.

The next afternoon, I snapped on the radio and heard on the news that the previous night, after we left, the lodge had burned to the ground.

Hank and I didn't go skiing anymore after that.

But it wasn't our most dangerous winter episode. That distinction involved Trusty Cruiser, the aforementioned VW in which Hank frequently drove Sue and me back and forth to school. On this one trip, taken after the Christmas break, the three of us were headed up to St. Mike's from our respective homes in Stamford. We were in Vermont, driving through the teeth of a snowstorm, when we approached the Williams River Bridge, which spans—how's this for a coincidence?—the Williams River.

A tributary of the Connecticut River, the Williams cuts through eastern Vermont and flows along Interstate 91 near Rockingham, where the bridge stands, a dizzying one hundred and thirty feet above the water.

Trusty Cruiser was cruising trustily along I-91 with Hank at the wheel, Sue in the back, and me, asleep, in the front passenger seat. Suddenly, the car hit a patch of ice on the deck truss bridge and fishtailed toward the guardrail. Sue, I was later told, gasped. Hank had a slightly stronger verbal reaction. I snored.

As the car slid toward an almost certain plummet off the bridge, Hank turned the wheel hard—either in the direction of the skid or away from it, I forget which you're supposed to do in a situation like that, and besides, I was asleep—and corrected the course of the vehicle mere inches from the rail.

"Oh, my God!" Hank exclaimed.

"Oh, my God!" Sue repeated.

"Hm?" I responded drowsily.

"We were almost killed!" Sue shrieked.

"What happened?" I inquired.

Hank and Sue told me the story.

"You missed the whole thing," Sue said.

"That's too bad," I mumbled.

"Go back to sleep," Hank suggested.

I did, dreaming the rest of the way to school of being in a flying car that wasn't called Trusty Cruiser for nothing.

In senior year, Hank got an off-campus apartment with a couple of other guys, but we kept in touch, meeting either at parties or in Burlington bars. We saw each other all the time after graduation, when he, Sue, and I moved back to our parents' houses in Stamford and started looking for jobs.

Sue found one at a bank (she would later go into education and become a teacher); I went into journalism (I started at my hometown paper, The Stamford Advocate, where I was a copyboy, a police reporter, a sportswriter, a city editor, and a features editor before achieving my goal of being a humor columnist); and Hank entered the business world (he began in sales and worked his way up the corporate ladder at several companies in a career that has been successful and rewarding).

By this time, Sue and I were dating seriously. When we got married, Hank was my best man. It was only natural because he had become the brother I never had.

A few years later, at a party at my sister Elizabeth's house, Hank brought a girl he said he wanted Sue and me to meet. I was in the kitchen, drinking a beer, joking around, and otherwise trying vainly to be the life of the party, when I spotted a tall, great-looking brunette. Right behind her was Hank.

"This," he said, when they had made their way through the crowd to where Sue and I were standing, "is Angela."

Just as I knew when I first spotted Sue in the cafeteria at Stamford Catholic High School that she was the girl for me, I knew within moments of meeting Angela that she was the girl for Hank. She was nice, smart, warm, personable, caring, and very attractive. Plus, she laughed at Hank's jokes. There was no question about it: This was a match made in heaven.

When they got married, I was the best man.

Because Hank has always gone where the opportunities are, he and Angela have lived in several places, including Roswell, Georgia; Northford, Connecticut; Branchburg, New Jersey; New Fairfield, Connecticut; Blacksburg, Virginia; Crystal Lake, Illinois; and Lake Wylie, South Carolina.

It was in Georgia, the Deep South, that these two Connecticut Yankees started a family. That's where their older son, John, was born. Chris came along five years later, after Angela and Hank moved to New Jersey.

Sue, the girls, and I visited the Richerts several times in Branchburg, both before and after Chris was born. Whenever we made our Jersey jaunts, the itinerary included outlet shopping (it's not a guy thing, but Hank and I went along because, let's face it, we had no choice) and the annual balloon festival.

"Nobody told us about the balloon festival when we moved in," Hank recalled. "I was lying in bed when I heard this roaring. I thought something was wrong with the house. It sounded like the furnace was going to explode. I got up and ran outside and there, about forty feet above our front lawn, was this hot-air balloon. The jet burner was making all the noise. It scared the hell out of me. I almost needed Depends."

We always enjoyed the balloon festival when we went with the Richerts. We never went up in a balloon, but, as Hank said, he and I could have powered one with our hot air. Sue and Angela didn't disagree.

Sue, the girls, and I visited Hank, Angela, and the boys when they moved back to Connecticut, but when they moved again, we didn't get a chance to travel to Virginia, Illinois, or South Carolina.

But we have seen them, just about every year, in what has become a holiday tradition: The Richerts go to Connecticut for Christmas to see Angela's dad, as well as Hank's sister, Janice, and her family, and set aside a day to take the ferry from Bridgeport to Port Jefferson, Long Island, so they can spend time with us.

Of course, every time we've see them, John and Chris have gotten bigger. "They started eating at a young age and haven't gotten out of the habit," Hank explained.

In fact, the boys—now great young men who are smart, handsome, and athletic—grew so much that they eventually went off to college. John studied business at the College of William & Mary in Virginia, after which he went to law school at Stetson University in Florida. Then Chris left home to study engineering at Clemson University in South Carolina.

"At that point," Angela said, "we were empty nesters."

"We've gone through three phases of our lives," Hank added. "BC, DC, and AC: Before Children, During Children, and After Children."

"They grew up so fast," Angela said wistfully. "Especially Chris. He was like thirty pounds at a year old."

"He was thirty pounds when he was born," said Hank.

"I remember how John used to jump out of his crib," Angela said.

"The projectile vomiting stories were the best," Hank chimed in.

So were the Santa Claus stories. Every year before Christmas, I would call John and Chris as Santa, and Hank would call Katie and Lauren as the jolly old elf who laughed when he heard them in spite of himself.

"It wasn't until John was twelve that he said, 'Santa sounds a lot like Uncle Jerry,'" Hank remembered.

Sue said, "Lauren thought Santa sounded like Uncle Hank."

"Hank says that since the kids left, we spend too much time having flashbacks of when they were little," Angela said.

For twenty-three years, Angela was a stay-at-home mom. "Somebody had to be there for the kids," she said. "It was a big sacrifice giving up my career, but I wouldn't have had it any other way."

Angela worked as one of the first female supervisors in the central office of Southern New England Telephone in Connecticut. When she and Hank moved to Georgia, she worked in regulatory services and human resources at Southern Bell until John was born.

"I did a lot of volunteer work when the kids were growing up," Angela said. "And I was on various PTA boards. Now that John and

Chris are out of the house," she added, "I'd like to get back into the workforce."

Nonetheless, just as Sue is in our family and Jane Lovelette is in hers, Angela is the backbone of the Richert family.

"She did a great job raising the boys," said Hank. "Fortunately, they didn't take after me."

"They have a lot of Hank in them," Angela corrected. "And that's good."

Like Sue and me, and Jane and Tim Lovelette, Angela and Hank still have a lot of their kids' stuff.

"We've moved seven times," Angela said, "but it just keeps following us."

Still crazy for each other after all these years, Angela and Hank finally have time to themselves.

"We've gotten to rediscover each other," Angela said. "It's almost like we're starting over."

Sometimes, when Angela goes back to Connecticut for a few days to help her dad, Hank gets bored being home alone.

"He now works from home, so he's there all the time," Angela said. "When I'm gone, Hank offers to do the laundry. I'll always say, 'Don't touch anything of mine!' He washed a sweater of mine once and it shrank so much, it wouldn't have fit a two-year-old. I'll only let him do the towels."

Is it enough to make a guy want to throw in the towel?

"No," Hank said. "I have it pretty good. Angela and I actually get to spend a lot of time together. We enjoy it. We watch reruns of my favorite show, 'T.J.Hooker,' with William Shatner. Angela will say, 'You're only watching it to see Heather Locklear, aren't you?' I must admit I like her. But now she's middle-aged, too."

Angela laughed. "We have our disagreements," she said. "But we clear the air and go forward. The communication is still there. So is the laughter. We love to laugh. That's important in any relationship, especially when you're empty nesters. And we see the boys when they come home on school vacations, so it's the best of both worlds. For Hank and me, it's a good time of life. We're still going strong."

Chapter 3

*You never realize just how empty the nest really is until
your kids get married. Katie had been married almost five
years before Lauren tied the knot. Twice. To the same guy.
As I've told people: Two daughters, three weddings. Only to
me could this happen. But it was all wonderful—
even some of the more difficult parts of
what turned out to be the trip of a lifetime.*

"Move Over, Steve Martin"

If Steve Martin doesn't want to do another "Father of the Bride"
movie, and the studio can't find anyone to replace him (original star
Spencer Tracy can't take the role because he is, contractually, dead),
I have just the man to play the lead.

I refer, of course, to myself. That's because I recently found
out that I am going to star in the sequel to my own version of the
popular series.

It gives me great pleasure to announce that Lauren is engaged to
be married to a wonderful young man named Guillaume.

The first time I was father of the bride was in 2006, when Katie
married Dave, who also is a wonderful young man.

It goes without saying, but I will say it anyway, that Katie and
Lauren are wonderful young women, primarily because they take
after Sue, who once again will be mother of the bride, the role
played by Diane Keaton in the two Steve Martin movies and by Joan
Bennett in the two Spencer Tracy movies. Maybe Sue should get an
agent.

Anyway, in the immortal words of that great philosopher Yogi
Berra, it's deja vu all over again. I'm thrilled because the first time
around was so memorable.

One part I will never forget, and which Hollywood could never top, was when Sue suggested we have Katie's bridal shower at home because it would, Sue said, "save us money."

"What a brilliant idea!" I responded enthusiastically, because as father of the bride I was already hemorrhaging cash.

"Of course," Sue added, "we'll have to redo the kitchen."

As you already may have guessed, we didn't save money. In fact, we spent more than my feeble mind could have imagined, not just on the kitchen, which was finished the day before the shower, but on our underground oil tank, which ruptured a week leading up to the occasion.

The tank was dug up, making the side yard look like a war zone, and was temporarily replaced by an old, rusty, above-ground tank that sat in full view of the guests, who gathered under a tent in the backyard. To add to the ambience, the replacement tank was festooned with balloons and a sign saying, "Congratulations!"

Still, the day was terrific. Not only were men invited, but it may have been the first bridal shower in history to feature cigars. It ended in a game of beer pong.

Because I have two left feet, which makes it extremely difficult to buy shoes, I took a dancing lesson so I wouldn't humiliate myself at the reception. Sue came along because she wasn't much better. In fact, we could have had our own show: "Dancing With the Stiffs." The lesson helped.

We also assisted Katie and Dave in picking out a wedding cake. The decision was made one morning at an elegant bakery, where we each had a slice of eight different cakes for breakfast.

And, a week before the big event, I pampered myself by going to a spa for a day of beauty, which included a pedicure, a manicure, and a massage. After all, sometimes a boy just likes to feel pretty.

It all culminated in the greatest wedding in the history of matrimony. Katie was a luminously beautiful bride, Dave was a dashingly handsome groom, and I didn't fall on my face while walking Katie down the aisle.

I'm sure my second time as father of the bride will be just as memorable. I might even invite Steve Martin to the wedding.

"Father-of-the-Bridal Registry"

Now that I am starring in my own sequel to "Father of the Bride," I have decided to take advantage of a perk I didn't know about the first time by opening a father-of-the-bridal registry.

I got the idea after talking with Bridget, who works at a bridal registry in a large department store.

"Men often feel excluded because the emphasis is, of course, on the bride, as well as the mother of the bride," Bridget said. "So I always say that if it weren't for the father of the bride, there would be no bride."

"And then the whole wedding industry would collapse," I noted. "So I guess we guys are pretty important."

"Don't tell your daughter or your wife," Bridget said, "but we couldn't do it without you."

That's what she told one father whose two daughters were getting married within six months of each other.

"He came in and I could tell he was stressed," Bridget recalled. "So he just decided to buy all the china for both daughters. I said to him, 'You are The Man!' That seemed to please him. Then I said, 'Let me make sure you get a free vegetable bowl.' It made his day."

Bridget, who said she loves working with her clients because they are there for a happy reason, especially likes fathers of the bride.

"A guy will walk in with his daughter and his wife and his daughter's fiance," Bridget said. "I can tell the father is a tagalong who was forced into coming. So I'll extend my hand and say, 'Congratulations. Now all I need is your checkbook.' Then I'll say, 'What does it matter? It's only money. Look at your beautiful daughter.' That softens them. I like to make fathers feel involved. After all, they're paying for everything."

Still, many fathers, as well as their future sons-in-law, are often clueless when it comes to items in a bridal registry.

"Some guys have no idea," Bridget said. "I have to tell them, 'With flatware, you eat. With stemware, you drink.' They don't know."

Since the emphasis is always on the bride, I asked, "Where can a guy go to open a registry?"

Bridget answered, "Home Depot."

So I went to the nearest store and spoke with Larry, who has been father of the bride twice.

"Yes," Larry said, "you can open a registry here."

Instead of china, which the store doesn't carry anyway, Larry suggested a cordless drill, a circular saw, and a tool kit.

"They'll make any guy feel special," said Larry, adding that the items are less expensive than most things in a bridal registry.

"The drill and the saw together are only $99," he said. "And the tool kit, which includes pliers, a hammer, and a screwdriver, is only $22."

As a practical joke on one of his daughters when she was getting married and had a registry at a department store, Larry said, "I told her to go in and ask for Doozy pots. The woman at the registry was Italian, like I am, and she told my daughter that 'doozy' means 'crazy.' My daughter came home and wanted to kill me."

Both weddings were wonderful, Larry said, though he added that neither of his sons-in-law had a registry at Home Depot. "One is an electrician who already had plenty of tools," Larry explained. "But it's a good idea for a lot of guys."

"What's the most valuable tool a guy can have in his registry?" I asked.

"A screwdriver," Larry said. "Of course, when the bills come in, you'll need another kind of screwdriver. But we don't sell those here."

"The Weddings of the Century"

Prince William and Catherine,
Duchess of Cambridge, St. James's Palace
Chapel Royal, Cleveland Row
London, England SW1A 1DH

Dear William and Kate:

I am writing somewhat belatedly to congratulate the two of you on your nuptials and to welcome you back from your honeymoon in the Seychelles.

I also want to thank you very much for being the opening act to the wedding of the century, the most magnificent event in Europe this year, and, if you will pardon the expression, a true crowning achievement.

I refer, of course, to the wedding of my daughter, Lauren, who is my princess, and her Guillaume, a prince of a guy, who were married in 1. on April 30, the day after your wedding.

They also had a lovely ceremony in the United States on June 5.

That means Lauren and Guillaume had two weddings and you had only one. I'm sure yours was very nice, although I had to read about it in the papers because I did not receive an invitation.

You must know that the Zezimas and the Windsors have had a chilly relationship since the Revolution, when an ancestor of mine, John Quincy Zezima, a columnist for the Colonial Advocate, wrote an investigative piece exposing King George's war plans, thus leading to the Empire's defeat.

The fact that my parents were not invited to the coronation of Queen Elizabeth or that my wife, Sue, and I were not on the guest list for the wedding of Charles and Diana is further proof of the chasm between our two families.

Naturally, I was hurt when Sue and I weren't invited to your wedding, but then I realized that you knew we would be otherwise engaged with the big event for Lauren and Guillaume. And since we knew the two of you were getting married the day before, we didn't send you, Charles, the Queen, or anyone else in your family an invitation, though I admit the courtesy would have been nice. For that, I apologize.

Still, I wish you could have been in France for Lauren and Guillaume's wedding, which was spectacular.

First, we went to the city hall in the charming village of Cadenet, the hometown of Guillaume's family, the Roberts. After the mayor officially married Lauren and Guillaume, everyone went up the hill to a breathtaking 900-year-old church for a religious service that was performed in both French and English and was unforgettably moving.

Kate, I know your dress was sensational, and was the talk of two continents, but Lauren's was even nicer. She was an absolutely beautiful bride. And Guillaume, in a classy gray suit that didn't have epaulets, was a handsome groom.

Later, we attended a fabulous reception hosted by Guillaume's parents, Martine and Pascal. It is nice to see that the Windsors and the Middletons get on so well. I am delighted to say the same about the Zezimas and the Roberts.

Martine and Pascal are wonderful. They welcomed us into their home the day before the wedding for a delicious meal, during which we talked, laughed, and got to know each other. Language was not a barrier. Martine's mother, who is affectionately called Grandma, won our hearts with her wit and warmth.

The Roberts continued their hospitality and generosity at the reception, the highlight of which was a slide show that was set to music and put together masterfully by Guillaume's younger brother, Frederic. It showed Guillaume and the Robert family through the years and included, of course, Lauren. There wasn't a dry eye in the house.

Throughout the day, we somehow managed to keep the paparazzi away.

While the two of you were in the Seychelles, Lauren and Guillaume honeymooned in Italy. When they got back, we had the American wedding, which was held at the Thatched Cottage, a lovely hall near our home on Long Island, New York. It also was a memorable day enjoyed by family and friends who toasted the beaming couple and treated them royally. You know the feeling.

Now that we are back to our normal lives, I just want to say that Sue and I wish the two of you nothing but the best. I am sure your family wishes the same for Lauren and Guillaume.

I hope this letter helps thaw the relationship between the Zezimas and the Windsors and that someday we can all get together to exchange wedding pictures. In the meantime, keep a stiff upper lip and give our best to the Queen.

Sincerely,
Jerry Zezima

"*Royal Response*"

On behalf of Prince William, an heir to the throne of the House of Windsor, which is in Buckingham Palace, and myself, an heir to the throne of the House of Zezima, which is in an upstairs bathroom, I am happy to announce that the centuries-old feud between our two families is finally over.

It was all a misunderstanding, as I explained in a letter I wrote to William and his lovely bride, Kate. I sent the letter to the royal couple, hoping but not really expecting to hear back. Imagine my surprise and delight when the following letter arrived in the mail.

> *St. James's Palace*
> *From: The Office of TRH The Duke and Duchess of Cambridge and HRH Prince Henry of Wales, Private and Confidential*
>
> Dear Mr. Zezima,
>
> The Duke and Duchess of Cambridge have asked me to thank you for your letter of 15th July.
> Their Royal Highnesses are grateful to you for taking the trouble to write as you did and were touched by your kind words of support.
> The Duke and Duchess of Cambridge have asked me to send you their warmest thanks together with their belated congratulations to Lauren and Guillaume.
>
> > *Sincerely,*
> > *Mrs. Claudia Holloway*

In case you are wondering, Mrs. Holloway, who signed the letter with a distinctive flourish in royal blue ink, is head of correspondence for the royal family, which receives about thirty thousand letters a year.

I don't know how Mrs. Holloway can still feed herself, much less sign all those letters, but I appreciate her response and the warm wishes extended by the Duke and Duchess.

Of course, we will have the letter framed and hung in a prominent place in our home, although it won't go above the throne because, God help us, it would be kind of tacky.

Now that the Zezimas and the Windsors are back on good terms, we can't wait until Prince Harry gets married. I'm sure an invitation will be in the mail.

"The French Connection"

I'll always have Paris.

Excusez-moi, s'il vous plait. I should say I'll always have Paris-Charles de Gaulle Airport, where I recently spent eight minutes (huit minutes) sprinting from one airplane (l'avion) to another during an otherwise magnificent (magnifique) and memorable (memorable) trip to France (la France).

My wife (ma femme), Sue (Sue), and I (Jerry) flew from New York to Boston, where we had a layover of more than five hours (cinq heures) before crossing the Atlantic (Atlantique) to Paris and then, after our mad dash through the airport to catch our connecting flight, which was boarding as we were landing, to our final destination, Marseille (no translation).

It was during this interminable journey that I completely mastered the French language (francais). Using a book titled "Say It in French," I memorized key French phrases (Ou sont les toilettes? Where is the men's room?) and words (au secours! help!), then practiced saying them with a nasally intonation that would have sounded better if I'd had a head cold.

Unfortunately, I fell asleep during the last hour of the transatlantic flight and forgot most of it, though I managed to get by without insulting anyone, which might have gotten me in trouble with the police (gendarmes).

Fortunately, and contrary to their unfair reputation for being rude, the French people were extremely pleasant (agreable) and helpful (utiles).

Whenever I didn't know what I was saying, which I can do in any language, I would ask, "Parlez-vous anglais?" ("Do you speak English?") The very nice person who knew I was a fumbling

American (americain) would smile, hold his or her thumb and forefinger an inch from each other, and respond, "A leetle beet."

Then that person would proceed to speak English with a charming French accent. To show my gratitude, I would speak English with a terrible French accent.

This came in handy when our luggage (les bagages) showed up two days after we did. I consulted my little phrase book for the proper reaction (not repeatable in either language) after being forced to wear the equivalent of a prison-issue T-shirt that was kindly provided by the airline. You don't know what a thrill it is on your first visit to a foreign country to wear the same underwear (les sous-vetements) for forty-eight hours.

My mastery of French also came in handy when eight of the nine people in our party got violently ill. The sole exception was me (moi). It was not because of the food. Au contraire! The meals we had in France were delicious (delicieux). Rather, somebody caught a stomach bug that passed from one person to the next until the toilette almost exploded.

"Je suis pas malade" ("I am not ill"), I told Bruno, who, with his lovely wife, Gielle, owns Hostellerie du Luberon, where we stayed.

"Pourquoi?" ("Why?") he asked.

"Vin rouge" ("Red wine"), I explained.

"Ha ha!" ("Ha ha!") Bruno laughed. "You have French blood!"

When everyone was feeling better, we went sightseeing. The South of France is like rural New England, with its rolling green (vert) hills and farms. Vineyards (see: vin rouge, above) are everywhere.

I especially enjoyed the markets in Luberon and Cadenet, where I purposely stood in people's way just so I could say—in French, of course—"pardon" ("pardon").

One day Sue and I got into our rented car (la voiture) and took a day trip to Aix-en-Provence, where we got lost thanks to the annoying woman whose voice, in English, was programmed into our GPS (Gallic Positioning System).

Her (for the 150th time): "Recalculating."

Me: "Taisez-vous!" ("Shut up!")

All in all, however, our trip was fantastic (fantastique). France is a beautiful country with wonderful people. Next time we go, we'll see more of Paris than just the airport.

Vive la France! Merci beaucoup. And, to anyone who was within earshot when our luggage got lost, pardon my French.

Chapter 4

My mother and father, Rosina and Jerry, Sr., and Sue's mother and father, Jo and Carmine, were empty nesters before Sue and I were. We owe them our lives, of course, but also the benefit of their example. My dad didn't live to see this book completed, but the others are still doing well. Meet the parents.

"Father Knew Jest"

One evening, when my sisters and I were young, we were eating dinner with my parents when my father suddenly complained that he had a splitting headache. "It feels like my eyes are about to pop out of my skull!" he moaned.

Then he got up and stalked out of the kitchen. We were all worried because my father never complained about anything.

A minute later, he came back into the kitchen wearing a pair of fake plastic eyeglasses, out of which, on springs, popped a pair of bloodshot Styrofoam eyeballs.

My mother, my sisters, and I burst into laughter. My father proudly joined in.

He had spent the day at work, fashioning these glasses that made it look like his eyes were popping out of his skull, just so he could play a practical joke on his family.

"What a guy!" I thought. I had always loved and admired my father, but from that moment on, he was my hero.

I grew up wanting to be like my dad, the original and best Jerry Zezima, because he was the funniest guy I ever knew.

One of his favorite stories involved his service in World War II. He was too humble to brag about his Purple Heart, but he did love to say that when he arrived in London, he got a letter from his

33

mother, warning him about all the seedy nightclubs she had read about in the paper. In the letter, she included the names of those clubs. My father smiled and told me, "They were the first places we went."

One night, when I was a kid, I was trying to get to sleep in my bedroom when I thought I heard my father crying. I got up, padded down the hall, and found him in the living room, crying—with laughter—while watching Laurel and Hardy.

"They were on a train," he later explained, "pulling people's pants down."

Thanks to my dad, I came to appreciate the genius of Stan and Ollie.

I also grew to revere other comic duos, like the Road Runner and the Coyote. My father and I watched their crazy cartoons, cackling as the Coyote's attempts to snare his avian adversary with a contraption from the Acme Company invariably blew up in his face.

We also loved another animated twosome, Sylvester and Tweety, the former a fumbling feline who hungrily stalked the latter, a little yellow bird who exclaimed, "I tawt I taw a puddy cat!" When Sylvester got his comeuppance, which usually involved an anvil, my father and I roared with delight.

Then there were Jackie Gleason and Art Carney, two other comic geniuses, who starred in "The Honeymooners," which my father thought was the greatest sitcom ever made. So do I.

My father and I were also a comedy team. I was the straight man. Whenever I called my parents after work and my father answered, he'd say, ostensibly with a mouthful of food, "We're right in the middle of dinner."

"Sorry," I'd reply.

My father would chortle and say, "I'm just pulling your leg! We already ate."

In some ways, we were comically different. He was the handiest guy I knew. Unfortunately, his skills skipped a generation because I am the least handy man in America. To me, a screwdriver is vodka and orange juice.

My dad was ahead of his time in that he was thoroughly domesticated. He bathed us kids when we were babies, he fed us, he did household chores. My mom said he never left his dirty socks and underwear on the floor. For me, it was another trait that unfortunately has skipped a generation.

One thing that I wasn't bad at, and at which my dad excelled, was sports. He played semiprofessional football as a young man and always found time to have a catch with me. He also took me fishing a lot. Once, when I wasn't with him, he caught a forty-one-pound striped bass. My mom took a picture of him with the monster, which he then gutted, cleaned, and chopped into fillets. Only afterward did he realize that he should have had it mounted.

"It would have been a great trophy," he said.

But the real trophy was my father, who died when he was ninety-three.

Mark Twain once said that there is no humor in heaven. That's not true anymore because my dad is there, laughing at the antics of Laurel and Hardy and playing practical jokes.

God, I bet they love the one with the eyeglasses.

"Mom's the Word"

When I was a kid, my mother wouldn't let me watch the Three Stooges. She was always afraid that I would go downstairs to my father's tool cabinet, get a hammer, and bop one or both of my sisters over the head with it. I'm not sure whether she was more concerned that I would hurt my sisters or ruin the hammer, as Moe frequently did when he used one on Curly.

I watched the Stooges anyway and have grown up to be a professional idiot, which, in retrospect, gives some validity to my mother's deepest fears.

But don't think she doesn't have a sense of humor. As my father did, my mother has always had a playful wit. She's also been quick to spot—and appreciate—life's absurdities.

When she was close to retirement from her long, varied, and rewarding career as a registered nurse, she called me one day with some astonishing news.

"You're not going to believe this," she announced. "The Air Force wants me."

She had received a notice in the mail from that service branch, which was looking for nurses and, doubtless unaware of her age, wanted my mother to enlist. Her name must have been on a nationwide database of registered nurses that the Air Force used to send out the notices.

"Will I have to go to boot camp?" my mother wondered.

To find out, I called the Pentagon. I identified myself as a newspaper columnist and a dutiful son who wanted to know why the Air Force wanted my mother. The person who answered the phone chuckled and transferred me to Lieutenant Colonel Janet Smith of the U.S. Air Force. I explained the situation and told her how old my mother was.

"She wants to know if she'll have to go to boot camp," I said.

"No," replied Lieutenant Colonel Smith. "But if she's in good shape and would like to get some exercise, she can come as our guest. By the way, has your mother ever flown a plane?"

"Not to my knowledge," I said. "But she's driven a station wagon."

"Close enough," said Lieutenant Colonel Smith. "Is she a good cook?"

"Fabulous," I responded proudly. "She can make anything, but she specializes in Italian dishes. Her spaghetti and meatballs are the best."

"I assume she makes the beds at home," Lieutenant Colonel Smith said. "How are her hospital corners?"

"So good that the sheets and blankets never come off," I said.

"Well," said Lieutenant Colonel Smith, "we'd love to have your mother in the Air Force, but she doesn't have to join if she doesn't want to." The officer paused and added, "How about you? Would you like to join?"

I gave the best reply I could think of: "My mother won't let me."

Lieutenant Colonel Smith got a tremendous kick out of the whole thing. So, of course, did my mother, who again displayed her deadpan humor when I was mistaken for the infamous Groucho Robber.

I used to take Katie and Lauren trick-or-treating while dressed as Groucho Marx. When they didn't want to be seen with me anymore, I started going out by myself on Halloween. Even without greasepaint and glasses, I bear a pretty fair resemblance to the legendary comedian.

Unfortunately for me, there was a spate of robberies in Stamford that were committed by a guy wearing a Groucho disguise—the fake eyebrows, nose, glasses, and mustache combo sold in novelty stores. During one robbery, the bank's security camera caught him in the act. The photo was plastered on the front page of the next day's Stamford Advocate.

That morning, as I was sitting at my desk, the phone rang. It was my mother. She didn't even say hello. She just said, "Please tell me that's not you."

My own mother! She and I had a good laugh over that. We felt even better when the real robber was caught shortly thereafter and, at least in the eyes of my mother, I was exonerated.

I caused my mom problems from the beginning: She was either hospitalized or bedridden at home for much of her pregnancy, which lasted almost ten months. When I finally made my grand entrance in the delivery room at Stamford Hospital, while a blizzard raged outside, I tipped the scales at eight pounds and thirteen ounces.

"You gave me a lot of trouble," my mother told me recently. "But it was worth every minute."

She said the same about my sisters, Elizabeth and Susan, who weren't as difficult as I was—who could be?—but who offered their own challenges to a woman who would have died for her children before they were even born, and almost did.

My father's death, while not unexpected considering his age, was nonetheless a blow to her. They had been married for sixty-two years, had raised three children with love and laughter, and had five grandchildren whom they adored: Katie and Lauren, as well as Susan's children, Taylor, Blair, and Whitney.

During my father's final illness, which lasted three months and followed nearly two years of physical decline, my mother displayed the same courage, perseverance, and love in caring for him that she did when she was pregnant with me and my sisters. It took a lot out of her because, face it, she was no spring chicken, either. But as she said about all the trouble I gave her before I was born, "It was worth every minute."

One evening not long ago, when I was up in Stamford on business and was staying at my mom's house overnight, she said, "When you kids moved out, we were happy for you, but we missed you. When you're empty nesters, you learn to make a life, to start over on a life of your own. Your father and I found other things to do. We took dancing lessons for seven years."

"Your feet must have been tired," I said.

My mother smiled and continued, "We also traveled, which we never did before. I was working and so was Daddy. He was always puttering around; he found a million things to do. There wasn't anything he couldn't come up with an answer for. His kids and his grandchildren were his world. They're mine, too."

"Sue and I know what you mean," I said. "We feel the same way about the girls."

"Even though you're empty nesters, if you're both working, you don't notice it as much," said my mother, who retired several years after my father did. "He had great foresight," my mom said of him. "He said, 'Don't get rid of the house. You never know when the kids might come back.' We've always had an open-door policy."

"Wouldn't you get a lot of flies in the house?" I wondered.

My mother nodded toward me and said, "Look who came in." Then she smiled again and said, "Your father and I were always happy that you kids were able to make lives of your own. In that respect, we felt we did a good job."

"Even with me?" I asked.

"Even with you," she said.

I guess watching the Three Stooges didn't hurt after all.

"These In-Laws Are No Outlaws"

I first saw my future in-laws in the parking lot at Stamford Catholic High School after Sue and I had attended our graduation ceremony. I kissed Sue, told her to have a nice summer, and said I hoped to see her in college.

"Who the heck is *that*?!" Sue's mother wanted to know after I strolled away.

"Oh, that's Jerry Zezima," Sue said casually. "He's going up to St. Mike's, too."

Sue's parents must not have felt too comfortable about that. But as my mother-in-law said many years later, "We cried when we brought Sue to college. She only knew Terri Rook," a high school classmate who also went to Saint Michael's. "But then," my mother-in-law continued, "she saw you and Hank Richert, so she felt better. We did, too. We knew Sue had friends up there and wouldn't be alone."

Their trust was sorely tested shortly after we graduated from college. Sue, Hank, and I went to our favorite watering hole, the now-defunct Sittin' Room in Stamford, for a Saturday night of conversation and conviviality. We all drove separate cars (I wasn't formally dating Sue at that point) and stayed until the place closed.

"I got in my car and started to drive home," Sue recalled when I spoke with her on the phone the next day. "As I was going up Long Ridge Road, I saw the headlights of this car behind me. I drove some more but the car was still following me. I was getting scared. I turned onto Cedar Heights. So did the car. Then I turned onto Clay Hill and the car was still behind me. It followed me all the way home and up the driveway."

"Who was it?" I asked anxiously.

"My father," Sue said. "He was livid. He was out looking for me. He wanted to know who I had been with. I told him I was out with you and Hank."

All was (eventually) forgiven and I started dating Sue. When we were married, her parents warmly welcomed me into their family, just as my parents warmly welcomed Sue.

No in-law jokes here. Sue's parents are wonderful. Like my parents, they have been loving, generous, and supportive. Family means everything to them. Whenever I get back up to Stamford by myself, either for a speaking engagement or to help my mom, I always stop by to see them. We'll have tea—or, even better, cocktails—and chat. Sometimes I'll help them with a chore, such as turning the mattress on their bed, which they can't do themselves. If I were up there every week, I'd have to turn the mattress every time. "It prevents lumps," my mother-in-law once told me. Sue and I turn our mattress once every six months, but I sleep better knowing my in-laws' mattress has been turned.

Like my mother, my mother-in-law is a great cook. Italian dishes are her specialty. She especially revels in making the traditional Italian Christmas Eve fish dinner. Calamari tops the list, and I love it, along with baccala, but I also have relented in recent years and eaten a dish I was never crazy about: angel-hair pasta with anchovies.

"The pasta is great," I used to say. "But I draw the line at fish with hair."

"Come on, Jerry," my mother-in-law would always respond. "Try some."

My father-in-law, who I think would eat it for breakfast, would invariably chime in, "You don't know what you're missing."

Now, after all this time, I do. And I think it's pretty good.

As my father was, my father-in-law is handy. I "helped" him put up a swing set in their backyard when Katie and Lauren were little. My main job was handing him tools. Afterward, I got each of us a beer.

"Thanks for your help," my father-in-law said.

I smiled and replied, "It was nothing."

My in-laws have been blessed with seven grandchildren: Katie and Lauren, as well as Sue's sister Cecile's children, Jordan and Vicki, and her brother Kevin's children, Andrew, Kevin, and Ashley.

Like my parents, my in-laws did a good job in raising their children. And, except for graduation day in the high school parking lot, they've always been happy to see me kiss Sue.

Chapter 5

It's bad enough that Katie and Lauren aren't living at home anymore. Now Sue and I—who used to have pets ranging from countless fish and innumerable gerbils to a dog and four cats—are down to just a couple of felines. If you think the nest is empty after the kids move out, try losing a menagerie.

"Lizzie"

There is an old and wise saying: The best things in life are free. Nothing epitomized that better than my dog Lizzie. She cost nothing, but she was priceless.

She came into our lives when Lauren, who was then twelve, brought home a little black and white puppy that a friend's neighbor had given to her. The woman told Lauren that if we didn't want the dog, she would take her back. Otherwise, she was ours.

Even though I love dogs, I was against the idea because we lived in a condo. Besides, the dog would have to be walked through rain, sleet, snow, and gloom of night. Guess who would end up doing it.

Approximately five seconds after I saw the pup, I fell in love with her. We fed her, took her to the vet for an exam, and adopted her.

Two weeks later, the woman called to say she wanted the dog back. Lauren was in tears. I got on the phone. Words were exchanged. Threats were made. A custody battle ensued.

Finally, in an effort to be fair, and mature, and reasonable, I told the woman I had veto power.

"What do you mean?" she asked.

"If you don't let us keep the dog," I replied very calmly, "I am going to call my Uncle Vito."

And that is how Lizzie became a cherished member of our family.

Nobody knew what breed Lizzie was—the vet wasn't sure and the dog wasn't telling—but we thought she was a mix of Lab, border collie, and terrier, with perhaps a little Italian from her adoptive mommy and daddy's sides.

What was clear, however, was that Lizzie had a prodigious appetite for lint, grass, acorns, cat treats—everything but dog food. She ended up on a special diet consisting almost exclusively of boiled chicken.

She loved her snacks, of course, which is why she grew into a full-figured gal.

Eventually, we moved from the condo to a house with a big backyard where she could run and play, though I still took her for walks. She quickly became the mayor of our neighborhood, greeting people with big, slobbering kisses.

She was, in fact, the kissingest dog I ever knew, even winning the Pooch Who Can Smooch contest at Puttin' on the Dog, the annual fundraiser for Adopt-a-Dog in Greenwich, Connecticut.

Lizzie, whose tail was always wagging, was both a canine alarm system (she barked at leaves that blew past the front door) and the burglar's helper: If anyone ever broke into our house, she would either drown him in kisses or help him carry out all our valuables.

She was the sweetest creature God ever made.

She also was half of an inseparable team whose two goals in life were to love each other and have fun. As the other half of that team, I can say we accomplished both in Lizzie & Daddy's Excellent Adventures, which were documented in numerous columns that ran in newspapers across the country and around the world. Lizzie also is in my first book, "Leave It to Boomer." She's even on YouTube. Lizzie became a global celebrity, but she never let fame go to her pretty head.

There was the time I had to brush her teeth. (Her breath sometimes smelled like a bean supper with the windows closed.) And the time, after reading about Sonya Fitzpatrick, TV's "Pet Psychic," I tried to determine if Lizzie had extrasensory powers. (Sue thought I was "The Pet Psycho.") And the time Lizzie actually beat me in a blackjack tournament. (I'm not playing with a full deck.) And the time I took her to New York City to meet Lassie. (The canine superstars got along famously.)

Needless to say, Lizzie was smart. I would have to spell out certain words, such as "car," "walk," and "play," because if I was talking to somebody else and Lizzie was within earshot, pronouncing them would set her off in a frenzy of excitement.

And she was tough. She twice tore an ACL, and both times, without surgery, she was back in playing shape in no time. Not like these rich, pampered professional athletes. Wimps.

Even when she died, a month shy of her fifteenth birthday, she showed a special grace.

But what Lizzie did better than anything was give unconditional love to Lauren and Katie; to Sue, also known as Mommy; and especially to Daddy.

Yes, it's true that the best things in life are free. Even if Lizzie had cost a fortune, she would have been worth it. She was the absolute best.

"Oh, Henry"

Over the years in my humble and frequently fur-flown household, I have been surrounded by women: one wife, two daughters, and various animals. The pet population has included a dog, four cats, two frogs, approximately one hundred and forty-seven goldfish, half a dozen hamsters, and too many gerbils to count because, face it, gerbils can't do math.

Of these many fine, furry, and finny friends, only one (to my knowledge) has been a guy. His name was Henry, one of our quartet of felines, son of Kitty, brother of Bernice, no relation to Ramona. He thought Lizzie, the dog, was his mother.

Henry was a mama's boy because he loved Lizzie and loved Sue even more. He liked his real mother, Kitty, but he had little use for me, his surrogate daddy and the only other male in the house, perhaps because he saw me as competition for female affection but more likely because I would get rid of the scores of eviscerated creatures (birds, rabbits, mice, squirrels, practically everything but the mailman) he left at the back door or, worse, wanted to bring inside.

Henry was a paradox: He was the most ruthlessly efficient killer I have ever known (not that I hang around with murderers, in case the police are reading this), but he also was the biggest wimp in the world.

And he was, indeed, big. I conservatively estimate he weighed two hundred pounds, give or take a hundred and eighty. He was like a small mountain lion.

Most of it was fur. His rich black and white coat was so long that sometimes you couldn't see his feet, which were armed with razor-sharp claws that left a scar on my left wrist from the time Sue and I attempted to put flea powder on him. It worked because I haven't had fleas since.

I'd say Henry was a Maine coon except he wasn't from Maine and raccoons were about the only fellow beasts he didn't count among his trophies. As a result, our yard—and, by extension, the entire neighborhood—was devoid of vermin. Not including me.

On the other hand (or, rather, paw), Henry was afraid of his own considerable shadow. We had him for twelve years, but just about every time he saw me or any other human besides Sue, he would cower and run away. I always treated him well. I fed him, I brushed him, I tried to do the male bonding thing.

"It's just you and me, Henry," I would say.

"Meow!" he'd shriek. Then he would make a beeline upstairs.

That was another thing about Henry: He sounded like Frankie Valli.

"What's the matter, Henry?" I would ask. "Is your underwear too tight?"

"Meow!"

Then again, he purred with love for Sue. He followed her around so much I was tempted to get a restraining order against him. If I fed Henry, he'd eat only a little bit and wait for Sue to give him more.

"He wants me to feed him," Sue would explain.

"Suppose you weren't around for a few days," I'd respond. "What's he going to do, go on a hunger strike?"

Between his critter diet and his regular cat food, Henry looked like he missed very few meals.

One thing he did miss, however, was Lizzie. They were inseparable. Henry loved to sleep right next to Lizzie, often with his head on her hind leg. He even took on the canine characteristic of giving the paw whenever he wanted something.

Henry hadn't been the same since Lizzie passed away.

Now he's gone, too. The house is a little quieter and, considering his size, a lot emptier. Sue misses him terribly. So do I. And although he wasn't a typical guy, a man's man with whom I could bond and goof off and do paw bumps and watch sports on TV, I have to say that, all things considered, Henry was the cat's meow.

"Maggie May"

Maggie came into our lives when Lauren left the nest. One of the first things Lauren did after moving into her own apartment was to get a dog, a seven-month-old black and white whippet mix she named, of course, Maggie. Or, as Sue sometimes calls her, Margaret, or Marge, or Margie, or Madge, or Mags, or some variation thereof.

Soon after Lauren got the pup, she called me to complain that Maggie was unburdening herself on the carpet. I was proud that Lauren asked for my advice because I have always had a way with dogs, even to the point of getting into barking matches with them in public. One of these days, Lauren, Katie, and Sue will have me declared mentally incompetent and put me in a kennel.

Anyway, it was not surprising that Lauren turned to me for expertise in such matters.

"You ought to ask Mom," I said.

"Why?" Lauren wondered.

"She trained you and your sister," I replied. "Compared to that, housebreaking a dog is easy."

I went over to Lauren's apartment with Sue, just in case further intervention was needed, and was greeted enthusiastically by Maggie, who showed her affection by using my hands, arms, and feet (but, thank God, no other appendages) as teething toys.

Lauren handed me the dog's leash, at the end of which was the dog. "Take her for a walk," Lauren instructed. "Maybe you can get her to do something."

"OK, Maggie," I said as we capered off. "You're going to do number one and number two, which adds up to number three!" At that exact moment, one of Lauren's neighbors came out. She immediately went back inside and closed the door.

Maggie and I walked around the large apartment complex several times. At one point, Maggie squatted directly over my shoe, but nothing happened. About twenty minutes later, I brought the dog back and wished Lauren luck.

"She'll get the hang of it eventually," I said. "Be patient with her. And buy some carpet cleaner."

It took some doing, so to speak, but Lauren finally got Maggie housebroken. This doesn't mean, however, that the little angel doesn't sometimes fall back into old habits, especially when she doesn't get what she considers the proper amount of attention. Or when you want to take her for a walk and try to put the leash on her by the door, where, in the excitement, she voids where not prohibited by law.

At such times, you're kind of glad Maggie doesn't wear pants. But she does occasionally wear other articles of clothing. In fact, when it comes to fashion, Maggie dresses better than I do. Sue made this disheartening observation when Lauren brought Maggie to our house so Nini and Poppie (what Maggie supposedly calls her grandparents) could doggy-sit. Maggie was wearing a little purple and gray striped sweater that could have gotten her on the cover of Vogue.

This wasn't the only outfit in Maggie's closet. Her wardrobe has included a polo shirt, a parka, and a raincoat. Lauren even bought her a Halloween costume so she could go trick-or-treating dressed as a fairy princess.

The most stylish thing in Maggie's garment collection is a tan Sherpa coat with a fur collar and fur trim (as if the dog doesn't have enough of her own fur) that Sue bought her for Christmas one year. Katie bought Maggie a party dress.

I don't have a Sherpa coat. My sweaters are old and worn. Same goes for my raincoat. I don't even have a party dress. No wonder Sue said to me, "Maggie has a better wardrobe than you do."

At least I am better behaved (most of the time) than Maggie. This was never more evident than the week before Katie and Dave's wedding. I was sitting in the office, trying to figure out how I was going to pay for everything without having to continue working even after I am dead, when the phone rang. It was Lauren.

"Dad," she moaned, "I think I broke my face."

"Are you all right?" I asked.

"No," Lauren said, sobbing.

"What happened?"

"I was walking Maggie, and she pulled me, and I fell face first into the bricks on the outside of my apartment. I might have a concussion and a broken nose."

It turned out that Lauren, who was the maid of honor, had neither, although she did have bumps and bruises that healed enough to be covered by makeup on the wedding day.

Fast forward to the night before Amy Lovelette's wedding. I got a call from Lauren.

"Dad," she moaned, "I think I broke my ankle."

"Are you all right?" I asked.

"No," Lauren said, sobbing.

"What happened?"

"I was walking Maggie, and she pulled me, and I fell down the stairs outside my apartment."

Lauren tore the tendons in her right foot and ankle and couldn't drive to Cape Cod for the wedding. She ended up in a cast and had to use crutches to get around.

Maggie took the rap for both incidents. She's really very lovable, in a manic sort of way. And she immediately took a liking to Guillaume when he came into Lauren's life. She's a mama's girl, to be sure, but she loves her daddy, too.

But Maggie is also—I say this with great affection because she is, after all, my own fur and blood—insane.

Whenever she visits Nini and Poppie, she chases squirrels outside and terrorizes cats inside. In fact, Kitty and Bernice have to seek refuge upstairs. I put their food, water, and litter box in one of the bathrooms and place a baby gate at the bottom of the stairs so Maggie won't go up there and create pandemonium. Henry used to taunt her, looking down from one of the middle steps and hissing at Maggie, who would respond by barking madly. Sweet old Lizzie simply tolerated her niece but clearly wasn't thrilled that Maggie got all the attention.

Still, we love our Mags. And she loves us. She's always happy to visit Nini and Poppie. But like any grandchild, she eventually has to go home. For empty nesters, that means the emptiness returns.

"I'd like to get another dog," Sue keeps saying.

"But hon," I always counter, "we're at a new stage in our lives. The kids are out and we're down to only two cats. Finally, we have a little freedom."

"I don't know," Sue will say. "It's just not the same."

Then Lauren will call to announce that she and Guillaume are going out for the day and won't be home until late at night, or are going on a trip for a week, and could Maggie please stay with Nini and Poppie.

Sue will hang up and say with a smile, "Guess who's coming to visit." For two animal lovers whose only grandchild is a dog, the fun never ends.

Chapter 6

A house is not a home unless there is something to do. And there always is. You would think an empty nest would need less work, if only because there are fewer people to mess things up. Then you could save on repairs. You would be wrong.

"That's All, Volts"

How many homeowners does it take to change a light bulb? Most people would say it takes only one—unless, of course, the homeowner is yours truly. Then I would need the help of a professional.

Not only couldn't I change the bulb in one of the two lights outside the front door, but I couldn't replace the fixture in the hallway. That's why I called Shawn Krueger, owner of Luminaire Electric in Yaphank, New York. Shawn came over for an estimate, quickly ascertained that I'm not the brightest bulb on the circuit, and said he would send over one of his best men, Jose Lucero, who not only would solve my problems but would give me a crash course in Light Bulb Changing 101.

At eight a.m. the following Saturday, Jose was at the front door, which I didn't realize at first because the doorbell didn't work.

"Basically," Jose said as he started to replace the fixture in the hallway, "electrical work isn't that hard."

"It is for me," I told him. "Maybe I'm not wired right."

Jose, who kindly ignored the remark, said that the first rule is to turn off the power where you're working.

"I'm usually asleep at the switch, but even I know that," I replied. "It's the rest of it that has me baffled."

I explained that I was actually able to change a light bulb in the fixture but couldn't get the cover back on because the screw wouldn't fully attach to the threaded stem, which was loose and couldn't be tightened. This wasn't surprising since the fixture was old and corroded (like me) and needed (unlike me, I hoped) to be replaced.

This necessitated undoing the wires, which I figured would be my undoing.

"All you have to remember," Jose said, "is that the white wire is neutral and the black one is for the power. In the middle is the ground."

"So we've reached a middle ground," I said.

Jose also ignored that remark and—after turning off the power, of course—showed me how to disconnect the old wires and connect the ones in the new fixture, which Sue bought after I couldn't get the cover back on the old one.

She also bought new outside lights. In one of the old ones, which also were corroded, the bulb had broken off and couldn't be removed without either a screwdriver or a pair of pliers. I let Jose do it.

Then I got brave and asked if I could try to connect one of the new fixtures. "Sure," Jose said. "Just make sure you attach the right wires."

It took a while—if I had charged myself by the hour, I couldn't have afforded it—but I finally managed to get everything hooked up. Then came the test. I flicked the switch. The light Jose changed went on. Mine didn't.

"You didn't attach the wires tightly enough," Jose said when he examined my work, "but at least you connected the right ones." He gave me a passing grade.

I was still a dim bulb, but at least I finally knew how to change one. That didn't help, however, when a fuse blew on what turned out to be a bad hair day.

This time, the electrical problem was caused by Sue, whose hair is much nicer and more manageable than mine, primarily because she irons it. Just so you don't think she puts her head on an ironing board and presses her beautiful tresses the way she presses her beautiful dresses, Sue uses a flatiron to straighten her naturally curly hair.

One morning, Sue was using the flatiron in our bathroom, which is the house's flatiron district, when she blew a fuse. Not only did the lights in the bathroom go out, so did the lights, the clock radio, and the ceiling fan in our bedroom, as well as the lights and the ceiling fan in an adjacent bedroom. We tried to restore power by flicking the circuit breakers in the fuse box, but nothing worked.

I didn't want to be kept in the dark any more than I usually am, so I called Shawn, who sent over—you guessed it—Jose.

This job was complicated because it entailed working with wires that, if crossed, could have electrocuted me, though my hair would have looked nice.

"You have to know what you're doing," said Jose, who knew I didn't. He added that even an experienced electrician can get the shock of his life if he isn't careful. That's what happened to a co-worker who was splicing wires.

"I saw him shaking," Jose recalled. "I thought he was joking because he has a good sense of humor and is always kidding around. Then he went backward and fell over, like a piece of wood. He was lying on the floor with his hands and feet sticking up in the air. He looked like a table that was upside down. I said, 'Are you OK?' He was all right, but he was really stunned. Since that day, he doesn't joke around anymore."

Jose wasn't joking when he told me that our problem was potentially hazardous because of faulty wiring. He traced the trouble to the next bedroom, not the bathroom, and said the wires were old. He fixed them in the bathroom and both bedrooms and suggested that we eventually update our entire electrical system.

He also suggested we go easy with the flatiron and the hair dryer.

"They use a lot of power," said Jose, adding that his wife, like Sue, used a flatiron to straighten her naturally curly hair. "Women spend too much money on their hair," he said.

When I admitted that I sometimes use a hair dryer, Jose said, "My father-in-law uses one, too. I always say to him, 'You mean you can't even go out without blow-drying your hair?' He says no. I don't understand it."

Jose, who has a full head of thick brown hair, said he didn't use a flatiron or a hair dryer.

"I use glue," he said, removing his cap to show off his spiked hairdo. "It's like a gel but stronger. In the summer, when I sweat, it drips into my eyes. Sometimes I don't even want to have hair."

"Maybe that's the answer to preventing blown fuses," I said.

"Our wives wouldn't like it," Jose replied. "That's why the electric bill is so high."

"Tell me about it," I said. "It's enough to make your hair stand on end."

"Magic Carpet Guy"

I have never been one to sweep things under the rug, mainly because I don't wear one. And I have never been on a magic carpet ride, mainly because all of our carpets are nailed to the floor. But I was floored to hear a carpet cleaner come clean about his crazy carpet capers.

Sue hired Dan Gallagher to clean some of our carpets because they were embedded with dirt, hair, and suspicious substances that I blamed on our cats.

"Your carpets aren't that bad," Dan said. "The job looks pretty easy, which is more than I can say for some other places I've been to."

Like the house that burned to the ground.

"I was outside taking a break when I saw smoke coming up from the back," Dan recalled. "Then I saw flames shooting from the roof. I rushed back inside and said to the homeowner, 'Lady, your house is on fire.' This angry look came over her face. I had already been there a couple of hours and she was still mad at me because I showed up late. I had other appointments and couldn't help it, but she didn't care."

As the fire raged, Dan asked the woman if there were any kids or pets in the house.

"She had three dogs and three or four cats that shed all over the carpets and the furniture, which is why she called me in the first place," Dan said. "I was like Ace Ventura, Pet Detective, rescuing these animals. One of the dogs tried to bite me. I had to coax another one out with dog treats."

The whole time, Dan said, the woman wouldn't help him.

"Then this guy came out of nowhere—I don't know if he was a neighbor or what—and tried to put out the fire with a garden hose," Dan remembered. "I said, 'Dude, that's not going to do any good.' So he disappeared. Then the fire department came. They put out the fire but couldn't save the house."

When it was all over, the woman reluctantly paid Dan for the part of the job he had completed. "I saved her and all her pets," he said, "and she didn't even tip me."

Neither did the twelve-year-old boy whose mother went out and left Dan in charge of her fourteen other kids while he cleaned the carpets.

"This woman had fifteen children that ranged in age from three to twelve," Dan said. "And she left me with all of them. There were diapers all over the floor. And one of the fuses blew—it was an old house—so I had to unplug the TV to plug my machine into that outlet. The kids had been watching 'Dora the Explorer.' They were screaming, 'What happened to Dora?' I called the mother on her cellphone—I don't know where she was—and she was yelling at me. She had some nerve. Worst of all, she never came back."

When Dan was done, the twelve-year-old boy paid him. No tip this time, either. As Dan was leaving, the three-year-old girl said, "Aren't you going to turn the TV back on?"

There have been lots of other kooky customers, like the woman who was growing marijuana in her basement ("It's a good thing that house didn't catch fire," Dan said), so Sue and I ranked among the more normal ones.

Dan said he would rank himself and his wife as pretty normal, too. They have two dogs: a Labrador retriever and a German shepherd greyhound mix.

"Must be tough to keep the carpets clean," I said.

"Not at all," Dan replied.

"Why, because you have an industrial machine?" I asked.

"Even better," he said. "We have hardwood floors."

"Sink or Swim"

Because I am a writer with only the lowest standards, there is no level to which I would not sink, no depths I would not plumb, for material. This column is a classic example because the laundry room sink became clogged with material I can't describe here. Drained after several pathetically futile attempts to solve the problem, I called a plumber.

Harry Strawsacker, the burly, friendly owner of Brookhaven Plumbing and Heating, showed up at precisely the promised time wearing a cap with a picture of a fish on it.

"You're a fisherman," I said. "I guess you can't stay out of water."

Harry nodded. "Fresh water, salt water, or dirty water, I'm always in it," he replied.

The dirty kind was in the sink, which is used primarily as a receptacle for soap suds and linty residue from the washing machine.

"We're only two people here," Sue told Harry, "but I'm always doing laundry."

The sink is also where I wash the litter boxes belonging to our cats.

"You've got a lot of stuff down there," Harry said.

I told him that I had tried to unclog the sink with three applications of a liquid plumbing product that had about as much effect on the clog as a bottle of beer would have on a bowling ball. Then I took a piece of wire and attempted to dislodge the blockage. The wire broke.

After that, I called a national plumbing chain for an estimate that rivaled the gross national product of Finland. I will not identify the company, but I am not a rooter of its roto service.

Finally, I phoned Harry.

"This job calls for an electric sewer cleaning machine," he said.

As Harry spun the contraption's long cable through the pipe next to the washer, he spun tales of his many plumbing and heating adventures.

"One guy called me at eleven o'clock at night because his bathtub was clogged up," Harry related. "I said, 'Can it wait until morning?' He said no because he wanted to take a bath and that my ad in the Yellow Pages said I offered twenty-four-hour service. I asked him how long the tub had been clogged and he said, 'About a month.' I said, 'Do me a favor: Rip out the page with my ad on it and throw it away.' Then I said, 'You don't have to tell me where you live because I'll be able to smell it.' Some people are unbelievable."

Like the woman who smelled smoke in her bedroom, where she had a fireplace, but didn't do anything about it for two weeks.

"She went to work one day," Harry said, "and when she came home, she saw that her house had burned down."

Then there was the guy whose home became a skating rink while he was wintering in Florida.

"His boiler blew and the house froze," Harry said. "The pipes busted and the water kept running. His car was caked in ice, the cabinets were frozen, and the floor had buckled. The guy called me from Florida and said, 'Meet me at the house tomorrow morning.' He took one look, handed me the keys, and said, 'Here, take care of the house. I'm going back to Florida.' You can't make this stuff up."

The worst people are the "weekend warriors," said Harry, adding that he often gets calls on Sunday nights from women who say, "My husband tried to fix the toilet and there's water all over the place."

Harry fixed the sink for a fraction of the previous estimate and, as a complimentary service, took care of a small problem in an upstairs toilet.

"Now," Harry said with a smile as he left, "your wife won't have to call me on Sunday night."

"Stand and Deliver, Then Run"

In all my years in journalism, I have never believed that you shouldn't let the facts stand in the way of a good story. But I do believe that the bare facts can make for the best stories.

That was reinforced when a couple of appliance deliverymen told me about the many customers who have answered the door in the nude.

Because I am modest, and didn't want to get into legal trouble, in which case I would have to wear court briefs, I was fully clothed when Armando and Julio came over to deliver a new microwave.

"People may think our job is boring," Armando said after he and Julio had removed the old microwave and installed the new one in the kitchen. "But that's not always the case."

Like the time they encountered a huge snake while delivering a refrigerator.

"We brought it to a house that was close to the water," Armando recalled. "The lady was very excited about her new refrigerator. But first we had to go down to the basement to remove the old one. This basement had two doors leading outside. We started to move the old refrigerator when a big snake came out from behind it. This thing had to be six feet long.

"Julio and I ran toward one door," Armando continued. "The snake must have been scared, too, because it actually jumped toward the other door. The lady screamed, ran upstairs, and went out the front door. She was in the yard, on the phone with her husband, saying she wasn't going back in the house until the snake was gone."

The snake got out, the woman got her refrigerator, and Armando and Julio got a good story.

But the naked truth is that the really good stories involve not snakes, which shed their skin, but humans, who expose theirs by shedding their clothes.

"The first time it happened," Armando remembered, "a naked woman opened the door. I didn't know what to say. I didn't want to look down, so I just kept making eye contact."

"Did she know you were coming over to make a delivery?" I asked.

"Yes," said Armando. "She got a call saying we would be there in about half an hour. You got a call, didn't you?"

"Yes," I said. "As soon as I hung up, I put some clothes on."

"Some people are strange," Armando said. "They know we're coming over and they don't bother getting dressed."

Armando estimated that he and his partner—sometimes Julio, sometimes another guy—have encountered nude customers ten times.

"And not all of them have been women," he said. "Three have been men. I definitely didn't look down then."

The first naked woman went into the other room to watch TV while Armando and his partner did their work, after which she paid them and they left.

"It was strictly business," Armando said. "But there was this one woman—she was beautiful—who answered the door dressed very professionally, in a business suit, when we came over to deliver a refrigerator. It wouldn't fit into the kitchen, so she had to get another one. We went back three or four days later and this time her husband wasn't home. Right after we got there, she changed into this hot outfit, with tight shorts and a very tight top. She wanted me to go into the bedroom to smoke weed with her and maybe do something else. I said, 'I can't do that, we're not allowed, and besides, I'm happily married, but thank you anyway.' You see some crazy things on this job."

Julio, also happily married, didn't have much to say, so I asked him if he liked his job.

"Yes," he said. "Except if there are snakes."

"Mr. Clean"

In my early days as a journalist, when newsrooms looked like landfills and the remains of Jimmy Hoffa could have been safely hidden from prying reporters who had the story right under their noses, my desk was so messy that it should have been condemned by the board of health.

Over the years, however, I have cleaned up my act. Now my desk is so neat that it looks like I don't do any real work, which I don't.

Still, it made things much easier recently when my colleagues and I moved downstairs. The man in charge of the operation, which seemed as complicated as the invasion of Normandy but turned out to be remarkably smooth, was building services manager Tom Perrotta.

"I've seen a lot of messy people," Tom said as we sat in his office, which was, of course, immaculate. "Some of them have tons of newspapers that you actually have to dig through to get to their desks."

"I don't read the newspaper," I said.

"Really?" Tom replied quizzically.

"Actually, I do," I said. "But we get it delivered. I leave tons of papers on the kitchen table until my wife bags them for recycling."

"At least you're not messy in the office," Tom noted. "One guy needed fifteen boxes to pack up all his stuff."

"I used only one," I said. "And I didn't even fill it."

"I noticed," said Tom. "It'll make it easier when you leave."

"Do you know something I don't?" I asked nervously.

"No," Tom replied. "But you are closer to the door now. Maybe we can put your desk in the parking lot. The only thing you won't have out there is climate control."

Tom knew which box was mine because it contained a picture of the Three Stooges.

"How come you don't have a picture of your wife and kids?" Tom inquired.

"I know what they look like," I responded. "But the Stooges are my inspiration. Besides, the photo of them adds a touch of class to my work space."

Speaking of family, Tom said he and his wife are very neat and that they have passed their cleanliness on to their sons, ages eight and three.

"My wife is neat, too," I said. "At home, I'm not."

"Sometimes, opposites attract," Tom said.

"If we ever won the lottery, we'd never collect the money," I said. "Either my wife would inadvertently throw out the ticket while cleaning the house or I'd put it somewhere for safekeeping and never find it again."

"How about your kids?" Tom asked.

"They're out of the house now, but the nest isn't empty because we still have a lot of their stuff," I said. "Once, when my younger daughter was home from college for the summer, my wife said her room was a disaster area. I called the White House to see if we could have it officially declared a disaster area so we would be eligible for federal funds to clean it up."

"What happened?" Tom wanted to know.

"The first lady's press secretary suggested we close the door," I said.

"If our boys play with something, they put it away when they're finished," Tom said. "The younger one is in nursery school, where they sing 'The Cleanup Song.' It teaches the kids to be neat."

Tom played the song for me on YouTube. It's pretty catchy, although I couldn't get the jingle out of my head for two days.

"You should pick up your toys when you're finished playing with them," Tom told me. "Be as neat at home as you are at work. I'm sure your wife would appreciate it."

I told Tom that my colleagues and I appreciated the fine work he and his crew did in moving us downstairs.

"It wasn't that bad," he said. "But we never did find the remains of Jimmy Hoffa."

"Diary of a Mad Storm Survivor"

DAY 1

Gray, wet, and windy. And that just describes me. It also describes Sandy, who is due at my house in a few hours. I put out a welcome mat. It blows away.

I am worried about two things: a skylight that would leak during a drought and a double-trunked oak that I am sure will fall on the house. At least it would give me hardwood floors.

Sue calls me at work to say Sandy has arrived.

"Don't let her in," I say.

Miffed at our lack of hospitality, Sandy knocks out our power and leaves.

Speaking of leaves, Sue says they are strewn all over the yard. So is a huge branch that has just missed the shed. But the skylight is not leaking. And the oak is still standing.

I can't make it home, so I stay in a hotel where the company has kindly put me up with several colleagues. One of them brings cheese and crackers and two bottles of wine. We play Scrabble in the restaurant. Words are suggested to describe the situation. None can be repeated here.

DAY 2

I shower at the hotel, which gratifies my colleagues when we return to the office. At the end of my shift, I go home to survey the damage by flashlight. Trees have fallen in the yards of neighbors on all three sides of us. For once in my life, I have lucked out. But we still have no power. Dinner is cold chicken I have to cut with a steak knife. Brrr appetit!

DAY 3

Halloween. Tricks but no treats. It is too cold in the house to shower, so I brush my teeth and go to work.

A female colleague says, "Your hair is neatly coiffed. What did you do to it?"

I reply, "I slept on it."

Sue, a teacher, is home because school is closed indefinitely. She drives more than half an hour to Lauren and Guillaume's house, which has power. Sue showers and does our laundry. Later, after we both get home, we have a romantic candlelight dinner: cold meatloaf. For dessert, there is melted ice cream.

DAY 4

I take the coldest, fastest shower of my life: one minute forty-seven seconds. Then I go to a convenience store to get coffee for Sue.

"Do you have gas?" a woman asks.

"I haven't even had breakfast," I respond.

I bring Sue her coffee and go to work. On the way back home, I stop at the Chinese restaurant next to the convenience store for a quart of wonton soup to go with the rest of the cold chicken. Yum.

DAY 5

Sue is sick.

"The Weather Channel should declare this house the cold spot in the nation," I tell her.

"Achoo!" she responds, adding: "I'm going to Lauren and Guillaume's. Meet me there later."

After work, I go home to pack a bag in the dark. Then I drive to a nearby gas station. I sit in line for more than an hour. When I finally get to the entrance, Joseph, who manages the station with his brother, John, says they are out of gas.

"Come back in ten minutes," Joseph whispers through my rolled-down window.

When I go back, Joseph lets me in and waves the other drivers away. John fills my tank.

"You are a good customer," says Joseph.

"And you and John are good guys," I reply gratefully.

I drive to Lauren and Guillaume's and have my first hot meal in days: Lauren's homemade chili. It is not chilly. But it is delicious. Sue and I climb into a warm bed and sleep like babies.

DAY 6

For the first time in nearly a week, Sue and I wake up not feeling like frozen fish sticks. The highlight of the day is waiting in line with Guillaume so he can fill his car's gas tank. I keep calling our house phone to see if (a) we have power or (b) a burglar answers. No power. No burglar, either. Still, there is no chance we are going back home.

DAY 7

Guillaume and I spend the day watching football. Sue calls the power company's hotline, which apparently is the only line the company has that isn't cold, to see if our house has power. It doesn't. We stay another night. I am beginning to feel like the Man Who Came to Dinner.

DAY 8

Sue and I get up early, thank Lauren and Guillaume for their fabulous hospitality, and drive back to our house, which feels like a meat locker. The carbon monoxide detector is beeping, so we call 911. The fire department shows up and determines it's only a dying battery. Later, Sue discovers that the battery in her car is dying. Our neighbor Ron kindly jump-starts it.

On the way home from work, I pick up a hot meal from the Chinese restaurant. Sue and I decide to spend the night in the house. I go out at ten-thirty p.m. to get gas. Two and a half hours later, I drive back home with a full tank. It's one a.m. I dress like I am going on an Arctic expedition (boxer shorts, flannel pajama bottoms, a T-shirt, a long-sleeve cotton top, a sweatshirt, sweatpants, and two pairs of socks) and climb into bed with Sue. We shiver ourselves to sleep.

DAY 9

Election Day. A nor'easter is coming. Bluster on all fronts.

At five minutes to six, toward the end of a busy day at work, the call comes from Sue: "We have power!"

I let out a whoop. My colleagues applaud. A chill (the good kind) runs down my spine.

I arrive home to a beautiful sight: lights. I enter to a beautiful feeling: warmth.

I think about all the people who have lost their homes or, worse, their lives. I know that Sue and I are lucky.

Good riddance, Sandy. From now on, the only thing around here that's gray, wet, and windy will be me.

Chapter 7

The nest may be empty, but it must be kept looking good.
And not just the outside of the house, but the property, too.
For me, it's easier said than done.

"The Height of Folly"

How much wood could a woodpecker peck if a woodpecker could peck wood?

Only a birdbrain would ask that question. So it should come as no surprise that it has been on my mind. It also should come as no surprise that my mind is in the gutter. This explains why, despite a paralyzing fear of heights, I had to climb up to the roof of our two-story Colonial, not just to reattach the gutter, but to battle a demented woodpecker whose mind—and bill—must have been in there, too.

The problem began when Sue and I were rudely awakened at six o'clock one morning by what sounded like machine-gun fire hitting the house.

"Whoever is shooting at us is a bad aim," I said drowsily.

"No one's trying to kill us," Sue replied. "That's a woodpecker."

Sure enough, we suddenly had a fine feathered friend that came back at the same time every day to serve as an avian alarm clock. Then we noticed that part of the gutter on the corner of the roof had come loose.

"It can't be," I said to myself, because Sue had already gotten up. "A woodpecker couldn't have done that."

There was only one way to find out: Send Sue up there.

"There's another way to find out," she said firmly.

So I got the extension ladder from the garage and, armed with a power drill and a set of gutter screws, started a climb that would have given a mountain goat nosebleeds. I don't like to be any higher off the ground than the top of my head. Unfortunately, the top of my head would have to reach the top of the house.

Complicating matters was a weeping cherry tree that partially impeded my long ascent.

"If I fall," I told Sue, "I'll be a weeping Jerry."

Life has its ups and downs. So did this project, during which I went up and down the ladder about half a dozen times, frequently getting entangled in the cherry tree's branches. I registered my displeasure in language that can't be repeated here.

"Hon," said Sue, who was watching this pathetic scene from the safety of terra firma, "you're talking to a tree."

Pretty soon I was talking to the power drill and the gutter screws, expressing similar sentiments because, like all inanimate objects, with which I have been waging a lifelong losing war, they wouldn't cooperate. Finally, I got a hammer and banged a new screw into the aluminum gutter, its vinyl backing, and the wood on the face of the house. For good measure, did the same with the loose screws (in the gutter, not my head).

While I was up there, I noticed some holes in the wood. I put two and two together and came up with twenty-two. "The woodpecker!" I thought. "Maybe now he'll go away."

I figured he wouldn't peck the aluminum gutter or the vinyl siding on the house, but just to make sure, I looked up "woodpecker deterrent" on Google and was directed to the website of the Cornell Lab of Ornithology.

Under "general woodpecker deterrents," there were tips for getting rid of the birds by tactile, visual, and sound means. Among them were aluminum foil strips, windsocks, handheld windmills, plastic owls, and an electronic distress call system.

"Instead of windsocks, maybe I can use my own dirty socks," I suggested to Sue.

"That would poison the woodpecker," she said. "Then you'd have to deal with the animal-rights folks."

I wasn't about to climb back up to the roof and hold a windmill in my hand. And I didn't want to nail a plastic owl to the shingles. I suppose I could have recorded myself doing a Woody Woodpecker imitation, but one of the neighbors might have called the cops.

So I put some aluminum foil strips up there. So far, the woodpecker hasn't come back. Still, I wonder: How much aluminum could a woodpecker peck if a woodpecker could peck aluminum?

Only a birdbrain would ask that question, too.

"The Dirt on Lawn Care"

Spring has sprung, and a young man's thoughts turn to love. Unfortunately, a middle-age man's thoughts turn to yard work, which he doesn't love. That's especially true in my case. The situation is so bad that I would put a "Keep Off the Grass" sign on my front lawn, but there isn't much grass to keep off.

So I went to a nearby Home Depot store to take a lawn-maintenance class.

The teachers were Frank, a lawn-care specialist, and Anita, a gardening specialist. The students were Susan, a new homeowner, and yours truly, an old homeowner who isn't a specialist in anything, especially lawn care or gardening.

The two most important things I learned in the class were: (a) have your kids do your yard work or (b) hire a professional to do it.

Since (a) my kids are out of the house and wouldn't do yard work anyway and (b) I can't afford to hire a professional (some, including my kids, might say I'm too cheap), I have to do it myself.

"My lawn looks like it was manicured with a flamethrower," I told Frank.

"Did you spread fertilizer?" he asked.

"I've been spreading fertilizer for years," I replied. "And not just on my lawn."

Fertilizer is very important for grass. So—surprise!—is grass seed.

"Water also is very important," Frank said.

"I prefer beer," I told him.

"I can see why you're here," he commented.

I'm glad I was because I found out that what I had already done—drop seed and then, a few days later, spread fertilizer—was, according to Frank, "totally wrong." He said, "You should do one or the other."

Anita agreed, adding: "Use a thatcher."

"You mean Margaret Thatcher?" I asked. "Considering her present condition, I don't think she would be much help."

After hearing this, Susan, my classmate, must have felt like a genius, though she admitted, "I just bought my house and I have no idea what I'm doing."

"Don't worry," I told her. "I bought my house fourteen years ago and I still have no idea what I'm doing."

But Susan and I got a good education from Frank and Anita, who talked about various kinds of grass seed, fertilizer, and soil. They also went over subjects such as weed and fungus control and showed us how to use tools such as spreaders and rakes.

"An iron rake is very effective," Anita said.

"I should use one to comb my hair," I remarked.

"You need a special kind with teeth," she noted.

"Will I have to bring it to the dentist?" I asked.

"No," Anita replied. "But you will have to bring it outside and use it to go over bare patches and mossy areas of your lawn." That, she added, will help grass seed take root instead of just sitting on top of the hard ground. Same goes for fertilizer, which should be spread in the spring, summer, and fall. The period in autumn just before the leaves drop is best for seeding, she said.

"Who does your lawn?" I asked.

"A lawn guy," Anita admitted. "But I seeded it first. My husband helps. My kids used to help—I have a boy and a girl—but they're in college now."

Frank said, "I have two teenage boys, but I do the lawn myself. It looks good."

I was so inspired by these two specialists, who said I graduated second in my class, that I am taking their advice: I will seed and fertilize at the proper times, water regularly, and set my lawn mower higher so the grass—or what there is of it so far—won't be too short.

In the meantime, I am going to put another sign on my lawn: "Keep Off the Dirt."

"Beating Around the Bush"

In "Duck Soup," the Marx Brothers' 1933 war satire, Groucho is reading an important document when he says to Zeppo, "A four-year-old child could understand this." Zeppo nods in agreement, at which point Groucho adds, "Run out and find me a four-year-old child. I can't make head or tail out of it."

That's the way I felt when I went to war with a butterfly bush that threatened to attack the house and I needed the help of a four-year-old child to defeat it.

The tyke was Brian Heidrich, Jr. His dad, Brian, Sr., who owns a landscaping company, came over with his crew to slay the floral monster that made Audrey II, the man-eating plant in "Little Shop of Horrors," look like a petunia. It was big enough to swallow a man (in this case, me) whole. It also drew so many winged creatures that our property often looked like something out of "The Birds."

Sue, who has grown several normal-size butterfly bushes around the yard, asked me to get rid of the big one so she would have room for a garden. It was a frightening task because the thing was about twelve feet tall and couldn't be transplanted. Its branches, which were more like tentacles, extended across the side yard and were within striking distance of the laundry room door.

At first I tried hedge clippers. The bush just laughed at me, although it could have been the wind. Then I got an electric trimmer. It was like using a plastic knife on a giant sequoia.

Finally, I called Heidrich Landscaping of Coram, New York. A few days later, a truck pulled up, followed by a car, out of which stepped the two Brians. I'm pretty sure Brian, Sr. was driving.

"This is Mr. Zezima," Brian said to his son, who was clearly unimpressed. But being a little gentleman, he shook my hand. Then he said to his father, "I want to help."

Brian, Sr. called over one of his workers, Luke Martinez, and asked him to give the young man something to do.

"Is he your assistant?" I asked Luke, who patted little Brian on the head and said, "He's my boss."

"Are you Luke's boss?" I asked little Brian. He smiled and nodded.

As head of the operation, little Brian supervised while Luke used an ax to chop down the butterfly bush. "Is Luke doing a good job?" I asked little Brian, who chirped, "Yep!"

To show he is not too important to get his hands dirty, little Brian helped cart away the branches, most of which dwarfed him. Still, he managed to drag a few of them to the truck. He also brought over a rake so Luke could smooth out the area where the bush had stood.

"If the bush hadn't been taken down, it would have gone through the door," Brian, Sr. said. "You could have had it arrested for breaking and entering."

Thanks to little Brian's expert supervision, there was no need to call the police. "You did a good job," I said to little Brian. He grinned proudly and replied, "I know."

Before the crew left, Brian, Sr. gave me a few pointers on plant and flower care.

"A four-year-old child could do it," I said. "And if I need help, I know just where to find one."

"A Bunny's Garden of Eatin'"

A wascally wabbit is wavaging Sue's stwaberry patch.

Sorry, it must be all those Bugs Bunny cartoons I watched as a kid. What I meant to say is that a rascally rabbit is ravaging Sue's strawberry patch.

The strawberries are the prizes in the various gardens that Sue has planted around the house.

She would never let me plant a garden because I have a green thumb. I think it's a fungus. I really ought to see a doctor.

Since we moved into our house, I have killed virtually every form of flora I have encountered. It's a good thing I don't know anyone named Flora or I'd be in jail right now.

I once had my own herb garden in which I grew parsley, sage, rosemary, and thyme. (I apologize if you can't get the song out of your head.) Herb, Sage, and Rosemary had a menage a twine, which I used to tie up the tomato plants in the adjacent vegetable garden.

It was pretty kinky. My deadly touch tragically put an end to their love nest.

It was, therefore, a pretty risky proposition when I asked Sue if she needed help planting flowers. Maybe it's because she had been out in the sun too long, but she kindly accepted.

"My Gerber daisies are doing very well," she noted as we began our work.

"Gerber? You mean like the baby food?" I wondered. "You must have bought them in a nursery."

I could tell that Sue regretted accepting my offer, but it was too late to do anything about it.

"I want to plant these flowers," she said, indicating the flats on the patio, "so you have to dig some holes in the bed."

"How will we get to sleep?" I asked.

Sue gave me a look that explained why the flowers are called impatiens.

I dutifully dug, but the holes weren't deep enough, so Sue took the trowel and showed me the right way to do it. "You can just hand me the flowers," she said. "I don't want you to kill them."

One thing that Sue trusts me to do is the watering. It is often my job to provide liquid nourishment not only for her flowers and herbs but for the strawberries in the side yard. They are sweet and succulent. Unfortunately, the rabbit thinks so, too.

"That bunny is eating all my strawberries," Sue lamented. "I don't know what to do."

"Why don't you put up a sign saying, 'Silly rabbit, strawberries are for people'?" I suggested.

"Silly man," Sue responded, "rabbits can't read."

Most mornings, when I am heading off to work, the rabbit will be sitting in the front yard, twitching its nose. Then it will look at me like I have two heads. Or one head with two very short ears.

One day I said, "Our friends have a pet rabbit named Stew."

The bunny hopped away.

But it didn't stay away for long. It came back later that evening, presumably for a strawberry dinner. Sue and I have actually grown fond of the little critter, so we don't really mind sharing our bounty.

It's a good thing I'm not responsible for the strawberry patch. The poor rabbit would starve.

"Branching Out"

For centuries, nature lovers and people with too much time on their hands have asked a perplexing and frankly ridiculous question: If a tree falls in the woods, and no one is there to hear it, will there be a sound? For weeks, I had asked an even dumber question: If a tree falls in my backyard, and I am there to hear it, will it land on my head?

I got the answer when a tree did fall in my backyard. It landed on the ground and did, indeed, make a sound, which wasn't nearly as loud as it would have been if the tree had landed on my head.

A few years ago, a large oak on the edge of my property fell on the house next door. My neighbors got the firewood, which I happily gave to them, not just because they were so nice and understanding (insurance paid for the damage), but because it would have been extremely dangerous to use the wood to start a fire in my house for the simple reason that I don't have a fireplace.

More recently, Sue and I worried about falling trees every time a violent storm was forecast. We also worried about the skylight in the family room. Skylights are nice when the sun is out, but essentially they are floods waiting to happen.

"If a tree fell on our house, and we were there to collect the insurance money, would we get a new roof and skylight?" I asked Sue.

"What a ridiculous question," she replied, adding: "Although it worked next door."

Storm after storm raged, we lost power, we lost food, we lost patience, but no trees fell. Then, one day, Sue noticed that a slender oak was leaning precariously, its branches almost touching the power lines and its roots coming up from the soggy ground.

"It's going to fall on the lines," she predicted. "You better call the power company."

Two days later, a couple of beefy guys came over to size up the situation.

"The company isn't going to send anyone to take the tree down," one of them said.

"Maybe you can take it down yourself," the other one suggested. "Do you have a chainsaw?"

"No," I said. "Just a handsaw."

"Get a rope, tie it around the tree, tie the other end of the rope around this other tree," the first guy said, referring to a larger oak several feet away, "and start cutting."

By this time I was at the end of my rope and was about to make a cutting remark when the second guy, who looked like Paul Bunyan, suggested all three of us try to push the tree over.

I felt like Paul's pal, Babe the Blue Ox, not because I'm as strong as an ox but because I'm as dumb as one, which I proved by saying, "Good idea!"

It actually turned out to be brilliant. We huffed and we puffed and we pushed the tree down. It landed far from my head. The sound, which we all heard, wasn't deafening.

"Now you're a lumberjack," said the guy who looked like Paul Bunyan.

"Or a lumberjerk," I noted.

After the men left, I got my trusty handsaw and, with the help of WD-40 and beer, started seeing that the sawing was easier than I thought. By the end of the afternoon, I had cut off all the branches, cut up the trunk, and dragged the whole kit and caboodle to the curb.

The next morning I could barely get out of bed.

If another tree looks like it is going to fall, and I am there to cut it down with a handsaw but am afraid it will land on my head, will I say the hell with it and call a professional tree service?

What a ridiculous question.

"He's All Wet"

A rolling stone gathers no moss—except, of course, for Mick Jagger and Keith Richards, who look a little green around the gills. But a standing house gathers moss—and it takes a lot of green to get it off.

That's why I shelled out $300 for a power washer.

I was prompted to make the purchase when a guy who does power washing on the side (as well as, presumably, in the front and back) offered to do the house for $400.

Sue, who is always thinking (of stuff for me to do), said we could save money if we bought a power washer and did the house ourselves. Or, more specifically, myself.

After God made Sue, He broke the mold. Now it was up to me to get rid of the mold with a new power washer.

I went to a large home-improvement store and spoke with a very nice, knowledgeable, and helpful sales associate named Frank, who knew that when it came to power washing, I was wet behind the ears.

"The proper attire for power washing is a bathing suit and goggles, but if you want an undersea effect, you can use a snorkel," Frank said after I chose a machine approximately the size of a Subaru, which was no coincidence because it has a Subaru engine.

Before I loaded the power washer into my car, which is not a Subaru, I got quite an education from Frank, a college business professor who has worked in landscaping and construction.

"I wear many hats, but not when I power-wash my house," said Frank, who added: "You're the first guy I have ever met who admitted that he doesn't know what he's doing."

According to Frank, guys think they know everything about home improvement, even when they don't, which is most of the time. But even if they're handy, they'll always defer to their wives.

"I'm pretty handy," Frank said. "But my wife doesn't trust me. We were redoing our home and we had to get his and hers shopping carts. When we got to the register, she kept everything in her cart and I had to empty mine. Guess who did the work. Me! And with the stuff she bought."

The house came out nice, said Frank, who predicted that mine would, too, because my power washer would get off all the moss, mold, and mildew and that, thanks to Sue, I would save money.

"The wives are always right," Frank noted.

I wasn't so sure when I got the power washer home and it wouldn't start. When I brought it back to the store, Frank started it on the first try.

"You have to pull the cord like you're mad at it," Frank said. "Swearing helps, too."

"I already tried that," I replied.

"And make sure the choke is in the right position," he advised.

"I'd like to choke the stupid thing," I said.

"Don't get *that* mad at it," Frank warned.

When I got the power washer back home, I swore at it and pulled the cord hard. It started on the first try.

Clad in a bathing suit and goggles, I posed as Sue took a photo, which will no doubt end up on a "wanted" poster. Holding the trigger handle and spray wand, I looked like either an action hero or a space alien.

When I pulled the trigger, a powerful stream of soap and water shot out. It splashed off the vinyl siding and soaked me.

"Are you having fun?" Sue asked above the din of the power washer.

"It's like my own personal water park!" I said giddily.

Best of all, the green on the side of the house started to melt away.

There's still more to do, but the place is looking much better. And, for what it's worth, I'm the cleanest guy in the neighborhood.

Chapter 8

If it weren't for Sue, I would have starved to death long ago.
Since becoming an empty nester, however, I've developed
an interest in the culinary arts. Here is what's cooking.

"Hot Stuff"

If you can't stand the heat, get into the kitchen. That's the lesson I learned after the oven lost heat in the kitchen and I couldn't stand the prospect of having to eat cold dinners until the apoplectic appliance was fixed.

Fortunately, Sue is at home on the range, otherwise known as the stovetop, which she uses to cook hot meals that sometimes include Stove Top stuffing.

The meltdown began just before Christmas, which we were going to host for thirteen people, two dogs, and me.

Enter a repair specialist named Larry, who examined the oven, performed all kinds of sophisticated tests, and came up with an unsettling diagnosis: "This thing is possessed."

I took his word for it—and added a few choice words of my own—because the lights kept flickering. It looked like something out of a horror movie. Even worse, Larry asked me several times to hit the circuit breaker, which I figured would either fry me or bake him, leading to the following spectacular headline:

Oven cooks repairman
Last job not well-done

I knew the situation was critical because the oven was running a low temperature of zero degrees. Normal is 350.

"I have to order a new control board," Larry said, referring to the electronic gizmo that runs the oven like the Starship Enterprise.

"When will it be here?" I asked.

"After New Year's," Larry replied.

When Sue heard this, her temperature skyrocketed. "How am I going to cook Christmas dinner?" she cried.

Even without Santa's help, the holiday meal was sensational because the smaller bottom part of the oven worked, as did the stove. Lauren and my mother pitched in by bringing food. Everyone—including the dogs—loved it.

A few days later, the board arrived, but we couldn't get an appointment until almost a week after New Year's.

Enter Larry again.

"You're back!" I exclaimed.

"Yes!" he said.

I knew Larry was the man for the job when he told me that he used to repair military equipment. "I did jet engines," he said. "In fact, I used to do everything. Now I'm an oven and dishwasher specialist."

"Sue has always said that no man in America knows how to load a dishwasher the right way," I told Larry.

"I don't even have a dishwasher," he said. "I wash the dishes myself."

"At least if your oven needed to be repaired, you could do it," I noted.

"No," he said. "I'd throw it out and get another one."

Larry also said he does most of the cooking at home.

"I can barely make toast," I admitted.

"My wife likes my cooking," Larry said, adding that he started when he was a teenager working in restaurants. "I specialize in Italian dishes, but I also do a lot of barbecuing. You don't need an oven for that."

Appliances have changed a lot in the forty years that Larry has been repairing them.

"You almost have to be a rocket scientist these days," he said, referring to the computer technology.

"It also seems like you're a doctor on call," I noted.

"Except we don't get paid like doctors," Larry said. "But I do have a lot of patience," he added, laughing at his own joke.

With the skill of a surgeon, Larry replaced the board and had our oven running like new. Then he printed out the bill, which came to $653.67. Fortunately, it was covered under the warranty.

"I'm very happy to get my oven back," Sue said.

"Me, too," I chimed in. "Now I won't starve."

"Maybe," Sue said to me, "you should learn how to use the oven."

Larry nodded and said, "Now you're cooking."

"Scrambled Egghead"

I've never had breakfast at Tiffany's, but I have had breakfast at Zezima's. And I can tell you from personal experience—because I'm the one who has made breakfast—that my eggs aren't all they're cracked up to be.

That's why I went to my favorite diner, CookRoom in Middle Island, New York, to learn how to cook eggs without having to scramble out the door and go somewhere, like my favorite diner, for a real breakfast.

Every Saturday morning, I make myself two eggs, often sunny side up but sometimes scrambled, especially if I accidentally break the eggs I am trying to cook sunny side up. I also have link sausage (if there are missing links, I use bacon) and either toast or a bagel, along with coffee and orange juice, though not in the same cup.

The meal is usually passable (no further explanation needed) but not really delicious. So I went to CookRoom to take a short course in short-order cooking.

My teacher was Roberto Benitez, the cook at CookRoom, which doesn't have room for a kitchen because it's a genuine diner that only has a griddle behind the counter. It's pretty hot there, but Roberto is always as cool as a cucumber.

"I don't put cucumbers in eggs," he said, "but you can if you want to."

In fact, Roberto's favorite breakfast isn't eggs. "I like Oreo pancakes," he said as he prepared an order of three regular pancakes that were the size of Frisbees.

"I've seen only one person finish a whole stack of pancakes," said manager Debbie Sweeney, "and it was a thin girl. Not even grown men can finish them."

"I can," said Roberto, who is a thin guy, "but I work it off."

He had to work pretty hard to teach me how to cook breakfast without either making a mess or burning the place down.

According to waitress Dawn Millwater, my order was "CR No. 1 up, rye," which meant two eggs sunny side up, with bacon, sausage, home fries, and rye toast, as well as coffee and orange juice.

"I thought my order would be 'JZ 911,' which you'd have to call after I made breakfast," I told Debbie.

"It won't be that bad," she assured me. "But just to be on the safe side, you won't be making breakfast for any customers."

As I stepped up to the griddle, Roberto showed me how to crack an egg. "One quick hit," he said. "Not too hard or you'll break it."

"Then the yolk would be on me," I replied.

Roberto handed me the second egg. I hit it against the side of the griddle. Nothing happened.

"Not too gentle, either," he said.

"I'm pathetically out of shape," I explained.

Then I hit the egg again. This time it cracked. I separated the shell and poured the contents onto the griddle. The eggs sizzled.

"You have to keep the griddle very hot," said Roberto, adding that I should watch the bacon, sausage, and home fries so they wouldn't end up frazzled.

I was frazzled trying to keep track of everything. When the eggs were done, Roberto handed me a large spatula and said to slide it under them. I tried, but the spatula didn't move.

"Harder," he said.

My next attempt almost sent the spatula flying. The third time was the charm. I slipped the spatula under the eggs and, without breaking the yolks, placed them gently on my plate, followed by the rest of the meal.

Then I sat down at the counter to the most delicious breakfast I have ever had.

The following Saturday morning, I made the same thing at home. It wasn't nearly as good as Roberto would have made, but at least I didn't have to call 911.

"You Go, Grill"

During barbecue season, I like to say that I am really cooking with gas. Unfortunately, that flammable substance not only is what my grilling usually produces in people, but it's not the best thing to cook with if you want to be a barbecue champion.

I got this hot tip from Phil Rizzardi, a barbecue champion who has cooked at the American Royal Barbecue Competition in Kansas City, Missouri, and the Jack Daniel's World Barbecue Championships in Lynchburg, Tennessee. He also has won barbecue contests in his home state of New York, including "Big Wiener" at Willie Palooza. His trophy is topped by the figure of the back end of a horse.

If that weren't impressive enough, Phil is the founder of BBQ Brethren, an international organization whose logo features the words "Brothers in Smoke."

Because smoke gets in my eyes whenever I barbecue, with the result that I either overcook or undercook whatever I am cooking, and I end up getting cooked myself by washing it all down with beer, I invited Phil over to my house for a private lesson.

"Wood chips are the way to go," said Phil, who brought his teenage son, James, a wood chip off the old block.

Phil also brought his grill, an old, rickety contraption on which marinated magic is made.

"Do you ever use this thing?" he asked when he opened my grill and saw that it was practically spotless.

"All the time," I replied.

"Let me guess," Phil said. "You knew I was coming, so you cleaned it."

"It was a little greasy," I confessed.

"That's OK," Phil said. "It's a flavor enhancer."

In barbecuing, grease is the word.

I told the champ about my first gas grill, which I had to assemble myself. "It took me a week," I said. "And then there were parts left over. I figured I would blow myself to smithereens, so whenever my wife wanted me to barbecue something, I made her start the grill. I felt like a mob boss who makes his wife start his car."

Eventually we got another grill, which came preassembled, but the ignitor conked out, so I had to turn on the gas and throw matches at the thing until I heard a big whoosh. Our present grill is a Lexus by comparison.

"A little kettle like mine may not look impressive, but it's better and it lasts longer," said Phil, who uses it when he gives barbecue classes.

"A lot of guys need classes," Phil said. "At a typical barbecue, a wife will marinate a steak, make potato salad, and set the table. Then she'll hand her husband the steak and tell him to hurry up and grill it. The steak will end up charred on the outside and raw on the inside, and the family will say, 'Great job, Dad. Call 911.' The poor guy doesn't know what he did wrong."

To do the job right, said Phil, a barbecuer needs a good meat thermometer that measures the temperature instantly so heat doesn't escape.

Also imperative is a chimney, a cylindrical metal holder in which to heat the wood chips.

"You can put paper at the bottom to get them going," Phil said.

This book would work nicely.

"Never use lighter fluid," warned Phil. "Don't put meat directly on the flame. And don't keep opening and closing the lid. If you're looking, you ain't cooking."

Phil, a technology analyst whose biggest barbecue payday was $3,000 (grand champions in national competitions can win up to $15,000), brought two hanger steaks, one to cook on his grill, the other to cook on mine. To help me along, he made a "smoke bomb," a handful of wood chips that he wrapped in foil, which he then perforated and placed in the corner of my grill.

"It'll help give the steak a smoky flavor even though you're cooking it with gas," he said.

When the steaks were done, we had a blind taste test. It was no contest.

"Phil's steak is much better than yours," Sue said. I had to agree.

"Next time you want me to barbecue," I suggested, "I'll invite him back."

"Rolling in Dough"

When the moon hits the sky like a big pizza pie, that's a mess. Or it would have been if I had tried to make my own pizza without the help of a pair of professionals who had me rolling in dough while creating a thin-crust pie that was, considering the lunar analogy, out of this world.

At a nearby pizzeria to pick up a takeout order (a large spinach and meatball pizza, my favorite), I asked co-owner Pietro Ribaudo if he would risk indigestion—better known in pizza parlance as agita—by letting me make a pie.

"Sure," he said. "And to minimize the risk to me and my customers, you are going to eat it."

A few days later, I stood behind the counter with Pietro and his pizza partner, Keith Lindblad, ready to make culinary history. Or at least a large spinach and meatball pie.

The first thing I had to do was put on a white apron, which actually was the hardest part. I fumbled pathetically with the string, trying to knot it behind me, until Keith kindly pointed out that it's supposed to wrap around and tie in the front.

Then I had to make the dough. Pietro, who was born in Sicily, took me in the back, where he instructed me to dump a fifty-pound bag of enriched, high-gluten, bromated flour into a sixty-quart bowl without rupturing a vital organ.

Next I put in three gallons of water, five pounds of semolina flour, twelve ounces of salt, twelve ounces of sugar, and three ounces of yeast. Then I set the mixer for nine minutes, during which I found out that Keith is of Irish, German, and Swedish extraction. "You don't have to be Italian to make good pizza," he said. To which Pietro replied, "But it helps."

When the timer went off and the mixture was dumped onto a flat surface, Keith told me, "Now you knead the dough."

"I could use a few extra bucks," I said.

"No," Keith responded. "I mean, you have to roll it."

This entailed taking a ball of dough, folding it over so there are no creases, and putting it into a small tin. The tins are refrigerated for a couple of days, so I had to make my pizza with pre-made dough, which was fine with me because if I had to wait that long, I would have gone hungry.

Back behind the counter, on a table in front of the big stoves, Keith showed me how to remove dough from a tin and stretch it out while tossing it back and forth from one hand to another.

"Contrary to popular belief," he said, "you don't twirl it in the air. I tried it once and the dough hit the ceiling fan, which shot it across the counter. It almost hit a customer."

Then I smoothed out the dough on the table while creating a ridge along the edge, after which I poured on the sauce, sprinkled on some cheese and oregano, and adorned the whole thing with spinach and meatballs. I put my pie in the oven and waited ten minutes. When it was done, Pietro, Keith, and Emily Werfel, who usually takes my telephone orders, all nodded approvingly.

"It looks delicious," said Keith, who put the pie in a box for me to take home.

"Mangia," said Pietro.

At dinner that evening, Sue said, "This is very good. The crust is nice and crispy."

Lauren, who had come for a visit, added, "You didn't scrimp on the toppings, either."

But the biggest compliment came from Lauren's dog, Maggie, who wolfed down a piece I fed her and, in begging for more, gave me two paws up. That's amore.

Chapter 9

As an empty nester, I have found that it's possible to be a man's man and a sensitive modern guy at the same time. All you have to do is grow a mustache, raise money for charitable causes, and go to a salon to keep yourself looking and feeling beautiful.

"Lip Shtick"

I may not be British, even though my favorite breakfast cereal is Cheerios, but for more than three decades, I have kept a stiff upper lip. That's because I sport a mustache.

I had never thought to grow one because mustaches are not common in my family. Two of the only relatives who ever had them were my Uncle Bill, who had a dapper mustache, and my grandmother, who wasn't dapper but had inner beauty and made a mean dish of spaghetti and meatballs.

The year after Sue and I were married, I had surgery to correct a deviated septum, which in my case was like repairing the Lincoln Tunnel. For more than a week, I was wrapped in bandages and couldn't shave. When the bandages came off, I had a mustache.

Sue liked the new look (anything was better than the old one), so I kept it.

I wore it proudly for years before finding out about the American Mustache Institute, an advocacy organization that is dedicated to "protecting the rights of, and fighting discrimination against, mustached Americans by promoting the growth, care, and culture of the mustache."

"We are the ACLU of downtrodden mustached people," Dr. Aaron Perlut, the group's chairman, told me over the phone, adding that AMI is "the only mustache think tank in the United States." Its slogan: "A mustache is a terrible thing to shave."

I quickly realized the immense value of the American Mustache Institute because, as I had long suspected, there is a lot of discrimination against mustached Americans. For example, the last U.S. president to wear a mustache was William Howard Taft, who left office in 1913. Perlut said that the last mustached major-party presidential candidate was Thomas E. Dewey, who did not, despite a famous newspaper headline, defeat Harry S. Truman in 1948.

Mustaches made a comeback in the 1970s, when, according to Perlut, "every man had three things: a mustache, a perm, and a turtleneck." But lip hair suffered a big blow in 1981, when, said Perlut, two things happened: "Ronald Reagan became president and ushered in a clean-cut, corporate culture, leaving mustaches to the fields of nail technicianry, motorcycle repair, and refuse disposal. And Walter Cronkite, God rest his soul, left the air. From that time on, it became unfashionable for TV newsmen to wear mustaches."

Now, however, mustaches are on the upswing. "When people like Brad Pitt and George Clooney grow them, it's good for the movement," said Perlut. "And the fact that Attorney General Eric Holder has a mustache is very important to our way of life."

To keep the momentum going, AMI hosts the Robert Goulet Memorial Mustached American of the Year Award, which is named for the late singer. That year's contest had a field of a hundred, including eighteen finalists, and drew almost 100,000 votes. The winner was Arizona Diamondbacks pitcher Clay Zavada, who sported a handlebar mustache. He beat out the likes of hero pilot Chesley "Sully" Sullenberger. I voted for journalism's only representative, hirsute humorist Bill Geist, whose neatly trimmed mustache gets plenty of face time on "CBS News Sunday Morning."

"Since you represent our way of life so well," Perlut said, "you should nominate yourself for next year's Goulet Award."

Because I am always up for a hair-raising adventure, I did.

According to AMI, the contest was the largest yet, with more than three hundred entrants. In addition to yours truly, the nineteen finalists included such notables as major-league baseball pitcher Carl Pavano, TV personality Pat O'Brien, filmmaker Morgan

Sperlock, North Dakota politician John Hoeven, and Washington Post columnist Gene Weingarten.

I also was up against two inanimate objects: Paydirt Pete, a cartoon mascot, and Carstache, a mustache for cars.

Of the more than half-million online ballots cast, I got about 85,000 votes, good enough for second place. For this unbelievable outpouring of support, I must thank my vast network of People With Too Much Time On Their Hands. My mother alone probably accounted for half of my total. I apologize to anyone who, as a result of constant computer clicking, has come down with RSI, which stands, of course, for Repetitive 'Stache Injury.

My supporters also can take pride in the fact that the Goulet contest raised money for Movember, an international charity that not only helps fund cancer research but encourages men to grow mustaches.

"Your performance was clearly admirable and your chevron mustache is very impressive," Perlut, the self-described "most ruggedly handsome man in America," told me by phone. "It was nice to see that your supporters came out in droves. You have quite a following."

But not as large a following as the winner, Brian Sheets, a firefighter from Osceola County, Florida, who got about 120,000 votes. He was honored at 'Stache Bash, which was held under the world's largest mustache, the Gateway Arch in St. Louis, where he received the coveted Goulet Award and a three-dollar crown.

"I'm humbled," Sheets told me when I called to congratulate him. "When my students at the Central Florida Fire Academy found out about the contest, they nominated me. Then friends and family started voting. It spread like wildfire."

It was the only fire that Sheets, who sports a Fu Manchu, didn't want to put out.

"I've always talked about the power of the mustache," said Sheets, adding that he will never shave his. "I burned it once, but I just trimmed the singed parts. I'd rather have my heart burned out of my chest than shave my mustache."

I don't know if I would go that far, at least not without calling the fire department first. But I do know what it's like to lose by a whisker. So it was with a sense of deja Fu Manchu that I got involved in another hairy situation when I attended the launch party for a reality TV series called "Whisker Wars."

IFC, the cable station on which "Whisker Wars" airs, hosted the bash at the Blind Barber, a New York City establishment that is part barbershop and part bar. According to the bartender, however, it does not serve gin and hair tonic.

The nice folks at the Blind Barber let me come in, though I have no hair on my chinny chin chin. I couldn't say that for the bearded boys of "Whisker Wars," a program devoted to what was described in an IFC press release as "the fascinating and hair-raising world of competitive facial-hair growing."

Yes, raising a beard, or a mustache, or a goatee—which is much less expensive than raising a child, because you don't have to put a beard through college—is now a sport. I felt right at home.

"You have a very nice mustache," said Phil Olsen, the founder and self-appointed captain of Beard Team USA and one of the stars of "Whisker Wars." Olsen not only has a mustache himself but a thick, luxurious, and extremely impressive footlong beard.

"I get compliments on my beard every day," said Olsen, a semiretired lawyer and a settlement conference judge in Nevada. "I've never heard anyone say anything negative about it. I'm sure some people don't like it, but they can keep their opinions to themselves or I'll send them to jail."

"I like your beard," I said.

"Thank you," Olsen replied. "You are free to go."

And go I did, straight to the mustache competition, which was being judged by three other "Whisker Wars" stars: Alex LaRoche, Jack Passion, and Myk O'Connor.

In a strong field that featured a variety of lip growths, I made it to the semifinals: a hairy half-dozen composed of five men and one woman.

Unfortunately, my chevron mustache, which was so successful in the Goulet contest, didn't make the cut.

That wasn't the case with Wendi Gueorguiev, an artist from Queens, New York, who made it to the three-person finals despite wearing a faux Manchu.

"Sorry," O'Connor told me, "but she has better qualifications."

They weren't enough to put her over the top. Still, Gueorguiev was pleased to be the runner-up, especially since, technically speaking, she cheated.

"There's a photo booth in the back of the bar," she explained. "I was trying on hats, mustaches, and beards. I decided to keep the mustache. I don't know what came over me. I made my way out front to the contest. I was surprised I finished second. I felt honored."

Gueorguiev, who declined to give her age but said she is "old enough to grow a mustache," commented favorably on mine. "It's pretty formidable," she said. "It's thick, nice, and lush, a little more masculine than the Dali-esque mustache that won."

But the winner was masculine, indeed.

"Hello, Dali," I said to him.

"Hello, Jerry," replied Max Baehr, a Web producer from Brooklyn, New York. The champ said he was inspired by his father, Tim, who isn't so much a Salvador Daddy as he is a whisker warrior.

"He has a beard," said Baehr, who waxed poetic about his waxed handlebar mustache. "My lady friend likes it," said Baehr, adding that he likes my mustache. "It looks great," he said.

Like all the compliments I've received about my mustache over the years, it wasn't lip service.

"How Now Waxed Brow"

I am not a highbrow kind of guy because, unfortunately, I am afraid of heights. So I will wax poetic, nostalgic, and, most important, analgesic about being lowbrow. That's because, for the first time, I got my eyebrow waxed.

Before undergoing this increasingly common masculine procedure, which women get all the time, I had, indeed, only one eyebrow. It was what is known in tonsorial parlance (a highbrow way of saying barber talk) as a unibrow, a strip of hair not unlike roadkill that extended from above the corner of my left eye to above the corner of my right eye. The left and right brows were linked by a hairy bridge that did not take E-ZPass. The result was one long eyebrow.

To achieve the desired effect of hair today, gone tomorrow (I told you I'm lowbrow), I went to see my barber, Maria Santos, who owns Charmed Salon & Spa in Miller Place, New York.

"More men are getting waxed these days," said Maria, referring not just to eyebrows but to legs, chests, and backs. It hurt just thinking about it. The imagined pain was excruciating when Maria described Brazilian waxes.

"They're like bikini waxes," she said.

"Guys don't wear bikinis," I replied.

"No," Maria said, "but some wear Speedos."

I got the idea, then started squirming in my chair.

"Don't worry," Maria said. "We don't do those here."

That was good to hear. Speaking of hearing, Maria told me about the guy who inadvertently got his ear hair waxed.

"He's a customer of mine, but he was on a business trip in California and needed a haircut, so he went to a barber who told him that he had a lot of hair growing out of his ears and asked if he wanted it waxed," Maria said. "The barber spoke with an accent and the guy didn't understand and said yes, go ahead and remove it. So the barber waxed his ear hair. The guy said it was the most painful experience of his life."

After hearing that, I was afraid to ask about nose hair. But I wasn't too skittish to ask for a brow treatment. Maria took me to a small room in the back of the salon and introduced me to Clara, a very pleasant and reassuring aesthetician who waxed rhapsodic about her job.

"I have been doing this for thirty years and I love it because I meet a lot of nice people, like you," said Clara, who asked me to lie back on a cushioned table while she got her tools, which did not, I am happy to report, include pruning shears or a Weed Whacker.

"I use tweezers, snippers, and a comb," Clara said.

Then she inspected my unibrow, which she said was "bushy but not unusual for a guy," and applied some analgesic soothing cream to soften the skin from which the middle part of my eyebrow grew. Next she got an adhesive muslin strip and pressed it to that spot.

"Ready?" Clara asked.

"Let 'er rip!" I exclaimed, instantly regretting my choice of words.

A second later, it was over. I listened carefully but did not hear a piercing scream emanate from my throat. In fact, I didn't feel a thing. Clara showed me the strip, on which was stuck a tuft of hair.

She then combed and clipped my now separate eyebrows, applied lotion to the newly bare area, and handed me a mirror. I no longer resembled either Groucho Marx or Joan Crawford in her "Mommie Dearest" period.

"What do you think?" Clara inquired.

"Beautiful," I responded happily.

Now that I'm the very model of the modern man, maybe a figure of me will go on exhibit at Madame Tussauds wax museum. I bet that'll raise some eyebrows, which is exactly what I did when I went back to Charmed for a dueling pedicure with Sue. It was for a fundraiser to benefit the Scoliosis Association.

When Sue and I arrived at the catered affair, which featured vendors who were donating their services, Maria introduced us to Nicole McConnach, a licensed pedicurist who didn't know what she was getting herself into. That was obvious when I showed Nicole my tan, navy, and white argyles and said, "I'm not wearing socks. The doctor thinks this rash will clear up in a few days. Still want to give me a pedicure?"

Nicole smiled bravely and asked what color nail polish I wanted.

"Well," I said, "the beach season is coming up and I want to look good when I dig my toes into the sand. I'd also like to impress the fish when I'm in the water. How about red?"

"Clear," suggested Nicole, who said guys shouldn't wear red, which Sue picked, or even black, which is considered a hot color.

"I guess red would attract sharks," I noted. "And black would make me look like I had some sort of foot disease. Clear it is."

The well-appointed pedicure room contained two plush chairs and all kinds of lotions, towels, and equipment—except, curiously, a gas mask, which I figured Nicole would need when I removed my shoes and the aforementioned hosiery.

As Sue and I settled into our respective chairs, rolled up our pant legs, and stuck our bare tootsies into small whirlpool tubs that were filled with hot water and mint-scented foot soak, Nicole asked who wanted to go first.

"Me!" Sue chirped.

"You can save the worst for last," I told Nicole.

"You have very pretty and delicate feet," Nicole said to Sue, who wears a size six shoe.

"Wait until you see Jerry's," replied Sue, who thinks I have the ugliest feet on earth.

"My shoes ought to come with oars," I said, noting that I'm a size eleven. "My feet look like two huge Limburger cheeses with really long toes."

When Nicole finished giving Sue the deluxe treatment, capped with an application of bright red nail polish, she turned her attention to me.

"Your feet aren't so bad," Nicole said as she examined them. "I've seen worse."

After Nicole applied lotion to my toes, she pushed back the cuticles with something that looked like a surgical instrument.

"What do you call that thing?" I asked.

"A cuticle pusher," Nicole answered. "It's all very simple."

She said that most men don't understand why women love to pamper themselves by getting pedicures, adding: "Usually, guys pamper themselves by buying more expensive beer."

After applying an exfoliant to my feet and calves, Nicole started buffing and rubbing until I exploded in a paroxysm of giggles that must have made the people out front wonder what the heck was going on.

"You're ticklish," said Nicole, giggling herself.

After she applied clear polish to my nails, I walked out front wearing the largest flip-flops in the salon to show off my glowingly pink feet.

"They look beautiful," Sue admitted.

For a donation of $10 each, Sue and I helped raise nearly $1,000 for the Scoliosis Association. The fundraiser was so successful that Maria said she wanted to have a benefit for breast cancer.

"I'll be there," I promised, sporting two neat eyebrows and ten shiny toenails. "And this time, I'm going to put the 'man' in manicure."

Chapter 10

*Empty nesters, start your engines. The kids are out of the
house, so your days of chauffeuring them all over town
until they get their driver's licenses, at which point they
start using your car, are over. But you still need a vehicle
to go to work and run errands. First, however, you have to
keep your cars running smoothly. And try not
to get into any accidents.*

"Crash Course"

If Sue and I wanted to have an impact on the people around us, we
would teach a crash course in driver's education. That's because we
have been in three crashes caused by people who had an impact on us.

The first mishap occurred when some idiot cut in front of me
at an intersection because his GPS told him to go the wrong way
down a one-way street. In this case, GPS must have stood for Guy
Positioning System, since the guy obviously was lost and, like most
men, wouldn't stop to ask for directions.

The second mishap occurred about a year and a half later,
when a little old lady pulled out of a side street in front of Sue's car
because, as the woman admitted, she wasn't paying attention. I can
only assume her GPS stood for Granny Positioning System.

The third mishap occurred only two weeks after the second one,
when an older man rear-ended Sue's car at a red light, damaging
her brand-new bumper, which she got as a result of the previous
accident. His GPS apparently stood for Geezer Positioning System.

I don't know what part of the country has the worst drivers, but
I do know this: Everyone on the road these days is certifiably insane.
Except for Sue and me. And we have the insurance settlements to
prove it.

To get a driver's education in the fine art of vehicular mayhem, I went to King O'Rourke Auto Body in Smithtown, New York, where Sue and I have had our cars repaired after each accident, and took a real crash course from manager Bobby Lombardi.

"The main problem," Lombardi said, "is that people don't pay attention when they're driving. Of course," he added with a smile, "it's not a problem for me because it's good for business."

There was one driver in particular who convinced him that auto body repair could be lucrative. The driver's name: Bobby Lombardi.

"I totaled a cop car when I was seventeen," he recalled. "I was driving a van for a printing company. There was a misty rain and this lady in a station wagon with kids in the back cut me off. I remember thinking, 'I can hit this lady or hit the cop car.' The cop had gotten out of his car to write a ticket, so I said to myself, 'I'll hit the cop car.' I hit it so hard that it slid and hit the car he was writing a ticket for. I jumped out of the van and said, 'Get that lady's plate!' The cop gave me a ticket."

After a few more mishaps, which mainly involved clipping taxis in New York City and putting a notch for each hit on his dashboard, "I decided to get into this business," he said. "I figured, at the very least, I could fix my own vehicles."

Lombardi, who has been in the business for more than thirty years, is now, by his own account, "an excellent driver." That's more than he can say for a lot of other people.

"They drive while they're texting or talking on the phone," Lombardi said. "Some people read the paper. I've seen women putting on makeup. It's ridiculous."

But the biggest causes of accidents, according to Lombardi, are GPS devices.

"They're worse than anything," he said, adding that he once got into an argument with his GPS. "It could speak different languages. I was looking for a place in Massapequa. The GPS said, 'Do you want to speak Italian?' I said, 'No! I want Massapequa!' It said, 'No comprendo.' I was actually talking with my hands to this thing, like a real Italian. I was yelling at it. Finally, I shut it off, went to a gas station, and asked for directions. I know guys aren't supposed to do that, but I had no other choice."

Lombardi and I, who are both of Italian descent, agreed that his GPS stood for Goomba Positioning System.

Lombardi, who has done wonderful work on our family cars, had this final piece of advice for drivers everywhere: "Pay attention. Don't drink and drive. And if you see Jerry or Sue coming down the road, get the hell out of the way."

"Massage at the Garage"

Early to rise and to the garage gets a man an oil change and a massage.

That new version of the old rhyme has been motoring through my mind since I found out firsthand (both hands, actually) that if your car needs work by a mechanic, your body might as well get a workout by a masseuse while you wait.

"It helps relieve stress when you get the bill," explained Rich Heins, a service adviser at Mid-Island Hyundai in Centereach, New York. The dealership had begun giving free massages to customers who might stall, overheat, or possibly even backfire as they contemplated the repairs being done on their vehicles.

"Are you going to put me on a lift?" I asked.

"No," said Heins, "but we will put you in a massage chair."

The stimulus program, he added, rubs customers the right way.

"And a lot of them could use it," Heins said, noting that one guy needed repairs for a problem that could have gotten him rubbed out.

"He said that whenever his car went over a bump, it died," Heins recalled. "So we looked at the car and found two bullet holes in it. One bullet hit the door handle and the other hit the harness and frayed the wiring, which caused the car to die whenever it went over a bump."

"It's a good thing the bullets didn't cause the owner to die," I said.

"I don't know if he was in the car at the time of the shooting," Heins continued, "but when I called and told him about the bullet holes, he said, 'Oh, yeah, I know about them.' Like it was an everyday occurrence."

"Still," I said, "that can make a guy tense. He must have needed a massage."

"Do you have any bullet holes in your car?" Heins asked.

"No," I replied. "But I need a massage anyway."

I got one from Sarah Chen, a registered masseuse who was waiting for me in the lounge.

I was her first customer of the day.

"You are going to enjoy this," Sarah said.

She wasn't kidding. After I had positioned myself so I was leaning forward in the massage chair, with my face sticking through a round opening in the headrest, Sarah began to work her magic on my neck, shoulders, arms, and back. I was putty (and a fair amount of flab) in her hands.

She explained Chinese pressure points, which she knows all about, not only because she is a thorough professional, but because she is from China. She also is very nice.

"Am I hurting you?" she asked as she used her fingers, palms, and elbows to loosen my muscles, which I keep in tiptop shape through a rigorous exercise program that generally involves walking to the refrigerator for beer.

"Mmmm," I responded happily. "Not at all."

"You're very tight in the neck," Sarah said.

"That's because I'm a pain in the neck," I explained.

Sarah then massaged my head, noting that I have hard hair and a soft skull.

"I always thought it was the other way around," I said.

Speaking of my head, Sarah said that rubbing a pressure point on my left hand, next to the index finger, can stimulate my brain.

"If I'm feeling stupid, which happens every day, I can rub that spot and feel smarter?" I asked.

"Yes," Sarah replied with a giggle.

The twenty-minute session was one of the most sensational and sensuous experiences of my life. I felt great from my head to my toes, even though Sarah didn't massage my feet. A good thing, too, because she probably would have passed out.

"Sarah was wonderful," I told Heins when he gave me the bill, which came to $101 for an oil change, a state inspection, an air filter replacement, and a left rear marker light replacement. "I don't feel any stress," I added.

"That's why we do this," Heins said. "Bring your car in for regular maintenance. And get a massage every 3,000 miles."

Sarah wasn't there when I went back, so I found another way to relieve stress: I asked a certified mechanic to show me how to change the oil in my car.

As a certified cheapskate, I knew I could save money if I learned how to do it.

"In a tough economy, every little bit helps," technician Naresh Ramjet said as we stood under my car, which was on a lift in the garage. "Besides," he added, "it's not that difficult, even for an amateur."

That, of course, would be me.

"You can't be any worse than the guy who hacked off the end of a spark plug and put it in the oil pan to hold the oil," said Ramjet. "Rule No. 1: Don't do that!"

As Ramjet showed me how to remove the splash shield and the filter, and how to drain the oil into an oil catch, Heins gave me another piece of advice: If you're going to pull a robbery, make sure your getaway car starts.

"This guy with a Corvette came in complaining that his car wouldn't start after he shut it off," Heins recalled. "So we left the car idling. Somebody came along, saw this nice car running, jumped in, and took off. He drove to a hospital, parked the car, went inside, and robbed the place. He ran back outside and jumped in the 'Vette. It wouldn't start. It was just going, 'Click, click.' There was a cop standing next to the door, tapping on the window. This idiot had the ultimate getaway car and he couldn't get away."

Service adviser Mary Husson remembered the time an older gentleman came in and said his car was making noises. "Nobody else could hear these noises," Husson said. "It turned out the guy had a hearing aid and he was getting feedback."

"Then there was the time a woman came in to say that her car smelled," Heins said. "It really did. The smell was awful. This was in the middle of a heat wave in August. The woman said the smell started about a month before. Apparently she had gone food shopping in July and forgot to take the groceries out of the trunk.

We couldn't do much about the smell, but we did take the groceries out. It's all part of the service."

Heins also recalled the man who complained that there were holes in the interior roof over the backseat. "I asked him who drove the car besides him. He said, 'My daughter.' We figured out the holes were made by pump heels," Heins said. "His daughter was doing more in the car than just driving. The guy's face turned beet red. He never came back."

I was getting quite an education in car care. Learning how to change the oil wasn't the most exciting part, but it was the most useful, thanks to Ramjet, a class A technician—the highest grade—who keeps up on technology by going back to school twice a year.

After he showed me how to replace the filter and put the splash shield back on, he lowered the car and showed me how to put in new oil and measure it with a dipstick.

"You may not qualify for a NASCAR pit crew," Ramjet said, "but now you can change your own oil. And you'll save money."

Said Heins, "I know this wasn't as nice as getting a massage, but you'll keep your car running well. Just make sure some stupid crook doesn't try to steal it."

"The Waiting Game"

As a motorist who has been driving (people crazy) for four decades, I am used to sitting in traffic for hours at a time. But I didn't think I would have to sit for part of two days when I went to renew my registration at the DMV, which stands for Department of Mass Vexation.

My adventure began on a Friday morning, when I drove to the DMV in Port Jefferson Station, New York, and found that, because of budget cuts, the place was closed. Instead of looking on the door for the office hours, which would have indicated the place was closed the next day, too, I went back the next day and found that—surprise!—the place was closed.

My keen deductive powers convinced me not to show up Sunday. So I went back Monday morning and beheld a scene that was something out of a Cecil B. DeMille epic.

"I'm sorry," said the nice woman at the front counter, where I was given number F-130, "but we've had a lot of layoffs and two people called in sick today. You're looking at a two-hour wait."

I sat down with about a hundred other poor souls in the hope that her estimate was wrong. After twenty minutes, I decided it was—the wait would be at least three hours. I left and came back even earlier the next morning.

Everyone from the previous day must have had the same idea because they were back, too. I went to the front counter and took a number. It was F-120.

"I think I know what the F stands for," I told the nice woman.

She smiled and said, "Good luck."

I sat down next to a guy who said, "I've been here for three days."

"Your family must be worried," I replied. "Did you bring a sleeping bag?"

"I should have," he said. "I showed up Thursday morning and the line was out the door. I waited a while and gave up. The place was closed Friday."

"I know," I said.

"I came back yesterday and the woman at the counter said it would be a two-hour wait," he continued. "I stuck around for about twenty minutes and left."

"Me, too," I said.

"So here I am for a third day," said the guy, who had number C-411.

A disembodied voice announced, "Now serving A-004 at window No. 4."

"We'll be here forever," I said.

A little while later, the voice announced, "Now serving C-411 at window No. 3."

"That's me!" the guy exclaimed. People around us applauded. I high-fived him. "It's like winning the lottery," he said as he scampered up to the window.

I sat from here to eternity, watching people text, surf the Web on their laptops, read books, or look at the overhead TV, which featured the Motor Vehicle Network. Programming included a game called "Can You Guess the Celebrities?" and a commercial for a law firm that specializes in personal injury cases resulting from motor vehicle accidents.

Finally, I heard the disembodied voice say, "Now serving F-120 at window No. 8."

"Yes!" I exulted as other customers congratulated me.

I stepped up to the window and was greeted by a pleasant woman named Dotty. I told her that I had been to the DMV recently to get my license renewed and that I was in and out in no time.

"Everything was very smooth and everyone was very nice," I said. "The DMV gets a bad rap."

"We do," Dotty acknowledged. "But we've been extremely busy lately because we are short-staffed. I hope you weren't waiting too long."

"Just a couple of days," I replied.

"That'll be $196.50," Dotty said. "Make out the check to DMV."

"How do you spell that?" I asked.

Dotty smiled. "Now you don't have to do this again for two years," she noted.

I nodded and said, "I can wait."

Chapter 11

*Since becoming an empty nester, I have been involved
in several criminal enterprises. Fortunately, with the
exception of a parking-ticket case, I have only had to
report for jury duty. After the kids move out, it's a great
way to spend your time, although it's not quite as exciting
in real life as it is on "Law & Order."*

"Law & Disorder"

As a law-abiding citizen, I am proud to say that I do not (as yet)
have a criminal record. On the advice of my attorney, who is in
jail, I can't say anything else except that I am disappointed I wasn't
chosen to serve on a court case when I was called for jury duty.

After I received my summons in the mail, I eagerly called the
telephone standby number every day for a week, only to be told by a
recorded message that my services weren't needed. At the end of the
week, I was excused and was told I wouldn't be called for another
six years.

I was so crestfallen at this miscarriage of justice that I went
to see Michael D. O'Donohoe, commissioner of jurors for Suffolk
County, New York, to find out why I wasn't picked.

"Don't take it personally," O'Donohoe told me as we sat in his
office just off the jury room. "We're looking for anyone who is
reasonable."

"I guess that's what eliminated me," I reasoned.

Actually, O'Donohoe said, failure to be called for a case isn't
unusual. "It happens," he explained. "At least you wanted to serve.
There are some people who will do anything to get out of jury duty."

Like the guy who filled out his juror information form by writing, "I hate everybody." Then he added epithets about various religious and ethnic groups.

"He thought we wouldn't pick him because he was prejudiced," O'Donohoe said. "He also blacked out his name and figured we would never find him. But he didn't realize there was a bar code on the form, so we tracked him down and put him back in the system. When he came in, he said, 'How did you ever find me?' I told him I had my ways. Then I reported him to the bias crimes unit. He wasn't anything but a knucklehead. In this job, you have to deal with idiots like that."

Even O'Donohoe's wife couldn't get out of jury duty.

"Not that she wanted to," he said. "During questioning for a civil case, an attorney asked if she was any relation to the commissioner of jurors. She said, 'Yes, I'm married to him.' The attorney said, 'You're his wife and you can't get out of jury duty?' My wife said, 'I'm sleeping with him and I still can't.' Then the woman behind her said, 'I guess my excuse isn't going to work.' My wife got picked. So did the other woman."

And if you think being a celebrity can get you off the hook, O'Donohoe said, think again. That's what actor Alec Baldwin found out after failing to report.

"He didn't show up for his first court date and he didn't show up for his next one, either," O'Donohoe recalled. "I said to his attorney, 'I am going to give him another date and I want him to show up this time,' but he didn't show up again. I called his attorney back and said, 'Let's not play games.' Finally, Alec walked in and said, 'I'm very sorry, Mr. Commissioner.' He wasn't selected to be on a jury, but he went through the process."

So did other Hamptons celebrities such as Christie Brinkley, Billy Joel, and Alan Alda, whom O'Donohoe called "a gentleman," adding, "He was a really nice guy."

There was, however, one person O'Donohoe did excuse from jury duty: his mother.

"One day a letter came across my desk," O'Donohoe remembered. "It said, 'My car can make it but I don't think I can.' And it was signed 'Helen O'Donohoe.' I said to myself, 'That's my mother!' So I called her and said, 'Why didn't you call me instead of writing a letter?' She said, 'I didn't want to bother you.' I get thousands of these letters, but I excused her anyway."

O'Donohoe, a former legislator, loves his job. "The system really does work," he said, adding that I wouldn't have to wait six years to be back in the county jury pool. "You can volunteer after two years," he suggested.

When I asked what I had to do to get on a case, O'Donohoe smiled and said, "Just make sure you're not the defendant."

Then he explained that in the criminal justice system, there are two separate but equally important groups: the attorneys, who prosecute or defend people accused of crimes, and the crooks themselves, some of whom are really stupid. These are their stories. They are all true. The names have not been used to protect the guilty.

"My favorite story involved a guy who was on trial for attempted murder," O'Donohoe told me. "The detective on the case was called to the stand and the prosecutor asked him what happened. The detective said the victim appeared to have been shot three times. The defendant, who had pleaded not guilty, turned to his attorney and, in a loud voice, said, 'He's lying. I only shot the guy twice.' The attorney said, 'Will you shut up!' But it was too late. His client was convicted."

What did the defendant in, aside from blatant stupidity, O'Donohoe said, was that he actually did shoot the victim twice, but because of an exit wound, there were three bullet holes.

"I think the defendant had a hole in his head," O'Donohoe said.

So, apparently, did the guy who stole a car so he wouldn't be late for court on a charge of grand theft auto.

"He pulled into the courthouse parking lot with a stolen vehicle," O'Donohoe recalled. "A check was run on the plates and it showed that the car had been reported stolen. Now this guy had stolen the car a couple of days earlier. If he had stolen it a couple of hours before he was due in court, it wouldn't have shown up on the report yet. So when he went in front of the judge on a charge of grand theft auto, for another car he had stolen, the judge asked him why he had stolen this one. The guy said, 'I didn't want to be late for court.' He was taken away in handcuffs." O'Donohoe chuckled and added, "You can't make this stuff up."

Another strange but true case involved a thief who ought to consider another line of work.

"This guy was charged with petty larceny," O'Donohoe said. "The assistant district attorney saw the police report and asked him why he stole the merchandise. Instead of saying he was needy or it was for his family or something like that, the guy said, 'I always steal things because I never get caught.' He wasn't the sharpest knife in the drawer."

Neither was the idiot who tried to pay his bail with the money he had used to bail himself out a couple of days earlier.

"I was down in arraignments when this guy was brought before a judge," O'Donohoe remembered. "He didn't have an attorney, so he was assigned one. The guy was charged with disorderly conduct, I think, and his attorney pleaded not guilty for him. The judge set bail at $250. Then the guy turned to his attorney and whispered something. The attorney told the judge that his client had already paid the $250. The judge said it was impossible since he had just set bail a moment ago. The attorney said his client wanted to know if he could use the $250 he paid for his bail two days before on another charge. The judge said, 'No, you can't use old bail money,' and then doubled the guy's bail to $500, which of course he couldn't pay, so he went to jail."

O'Donohoe said that while criminal stupidity certainly isn't limited to Suffolk County, he has enough crazy stories for a TV show.

"If the producers of 'Law & Order' want some funny storylines," O'Donohoe said, "they ought to come here."

"Jerry Duty"

It was an offer I couldn't refuse: Report to jury duty for a mob trial or wake up next to a horse's head. Sue, who wakes up every morning next to the other end of a horse, said it would be safer to do my civic duty than to end up on trial myself.

So I drove to the United States District Court in Brooklyn, New York, to see if I would be selected to sit on the jury for the trial of two alleged mobsters who were charged with murder, robbery, extortion, and—perhaps the most serious offense—having silly nicknames.

I was one of about two hundred and twenty-five prospective jurors in a pool of more than four hundred. I don't know what happened to the others (maybe they're in the witness protection program), but our group had to sit around so long that we could have watched three episodes of "Law & Order."

Finally, we were led from the juror waiting area to a long hallway where we were told to break into double file. Then we had to step up to a table at which two jury administrators gave us juror numbers (mine was 390) and told each of us to take a pencil, which we would later use to fill out a questionnaire.

"If I keep the pencil, will I get nabbed for stealing?" I asked one of the administrators.

"It's the property of the federal government," she replied, pleasantly but firmly. "You have to return it on your way out."

My grand larceny case would have to wait because I was on my way into a courtroom so large, it could have hosted a Hollywood premiere.

"Am I going to see a movie?" I asked deputy court clerk Melissa Burke, who ushered me into the second row.

"No," she said, "but you will be entertained."

Burke turned out to be so entertaining that she should be in Hollywood.

"Welcome to U.S. District Court," she said. "We're very happy to see you."

Burke instructed us to stand and raise our right hands so we could be sworn in.

"This is a criminal trial," she continued. "It could last ten weeks. You will be reimbursed for your travel expenses. Make sure you get parking and bridge receipts. Don't worry about figuring out mileage. We'll do that. We're the feds. We know where you live."

When someone asked if the trial would be held on weekends, Burke replied, "No. The judge has a life. I have a life. We won't sequester you. We're not here to put you up in a hotel. Don't think we're going to give you the keys to a suite at the Marriott. You have to go back home to your spouses whether you like it or not."

A woman raised her hand and said, "I'm pregnant."

"Congratulations," said Burke. "You can put that down under hardship."

"I might try that excuse myself," I said to the person sitting next to me. Then I raised my hand and asked, "How come you don't have your own talk show?"

Burke smiled and said, "People have asked me that, but it's not my passion. I want to be a lawyer."

A guy in the back muttered, "My condolences."

Before each of us filled out a forty-three-page questionnaire, Burke said those of us who were called back would have to report the following week.

"Don't tell your boss that you have to report for the rest of this week and then go to Atlantic City or Las Vegas," she warned. "Your employers will be calling us. We will tell them the truth."

After filling out the questionnaire, I returned my pencil to the jury administrator and went straight home. I was called back but wasn't selected to sit on the jury.

"Thank you for serving," Burke told me.

"You're welcome," I said. "Here's my verdict: Get an agent. And if you're ever an attorney on 'Law & Order,' I want to be one of the jurors."

"That's the Ticket"

I am not a lawyer, although I have been admitted to many bars, but at the risk of being sentenced to life in prison for felonious stupidity, I decided to represent myself when I went to traffic court to fight a parking ticket.

I got it when I drove with Sue and Lauren to the Port Jefferson train station for a trip to New York, New York, it's a hell of a town, the city that never sleeps, a place where I could be king of the hill, top of the heap, and come back to find a $100 ticket on the windshield of my car.

The problem was that I couldn't find a parking space at the train station, so I parked in an adjacent lot I thought was affiliated with the station. It wasn't.

The Zezimas took Manhattan (and politely gave it back after spending considerably more than the original $24 selling price), then returned to find the parking ticket. About three weeks later, I got a piece of mail that read:

Re: Vehicle plate number JZEE

OFFICIAL NOTICE You are hereby ordered to appear for a conference at:

PORT JEFFERSON VILLAGE COURT to determine the final disposition of the outstanding summons(es) issued to the above-mentioned vehicle plate number. Failure to appear will result in rendering a default judgment.

Since it was not the fault of my judgment, rendering me innocent, I didn't fail to appear in court at the mandated time of seven p.m. Neither did about a hundred other people, who were there for parking tickets, moving violations, and various misdemeanors.

It was standing room only, so it was not asking too much for me to stand, which I was already doing, as the Hon. John F. Reilly entered the courtroom.

Judge Reilly, who was indeed honorable, opened the proceedings by explaining that defendants could either plead guilty or ask for a conference with the district attorney. This, he said, could result in a subsequent guilty plea with the possibility of a reduced fine or a trial to be held at a later date.

I imagined my case going all the way to the Supreme Court—for a parking ticket. My reverie was interrupted when Judge Reilly called my name.

"How do you plead?" he asked as I stood before him.

"Clueless, your honor," I replied.

"Clueless is not an option," Judge Reilly said. "You have to plead either guilty or not guilty."

"Not guilty," I said firmly.

I was instructed to sit down, if I could find a seat, and wait for my conference with the DA. About ten minutes later, I was called over by Dara Martin, the village prosecutor, who also was honorable. I was about to explain why I was so clueless in my failure to notice signs in the parking lot next to the train station (it's for a residential complex) when she said I had two parking tickets.

"The first is from 2006," prosecutor Martin said, showing me the ticket. "It's for a black Chevy Suburban and it has your plate number, JZEE."

"My wife got me the plate because she said I had that name before Jay-Z," I said, "but it was only three or four years ago. And I have never driven a black Chevy Suburban. I have a gold Hyundai Santa Fe."

Since the ticket was several years old, the cost would have been in the hundreds of dollars, said prosecutor Martin, who tossed it out and asked me to explain the cluelessness that led to the second ticket.

"OK," she said, going easy on me. "I'll reduce it to $40 if you plead guilty."

"Guilty as charged," I said. "Now I don't have to go to the Supreme Court."

Chapter 12

A lot of empty nesters recall the days when their kids had braces. Now some parents who didn't have braces when they were kids are getting them. The difference is that they're the kind other people can't see. That's something to smile about, though you still want to frown when your spouse won't put the cap back on the toothpaste.

"Brace Yourself"

I have often been told, generally by people who need glasses, that I have a nice smile. I don't know how they can tell because these same people are always saying that whenever I open my mouth, I put my foot in it.

That's why, in my mid-fifties, I wanted to get something straight: my teeth.

A couple of my pearly whites—one on the top, one on the bottom—had begun to wander. This is what my mind frequently does. At such times, my eyes will glaze over and I will break into a goofy grin that used to expose twenty-six flawless teeth, as well as the two crooked ones that apparently had been pushed out of alignment by my size eleven foot.

To correct my dental dilemma, I decided to get braces.

This is not uncommon among baby boomers who, like me, did not have braces when they were young. How well I remember my unfortunate classmates who answered to the name "metal-mouth" and were warned, by sympathetic friends such as myself, to watch out for flying magnets.

Sue didn't have braces when she was a kid and her teeth are beautiful. Same goes for Katie and Lauren, who saved me a fortune in orthodontic work. (I have spent a fortune on them anyway, but that's another story.)

Back in those days, however, there was no such thing as "invisible braces," which go by the brand name Invisalign. They are made of plastic, not metal, and aren't detectable to people who think you have a nice smile.

To find out if I qualified, I went for a consultation to the Dental Care Center at Stony Brook University, which is close to my house on Long Island and has an excellent reputation as a teaching facility.

Dr. Ben Murray, an orthodontic resident, was assigned to straighten out the situation.

"Did you have braces when you were a kid?" I asked.

"Yes," Dr. Murray replied. "For four months. I was in fifth grade and I was a horrible patient for my father, who's a dentist. I wouldn't come in for appointments. Finally, I had enough of braces and asked my father to take them off."

"Are they that bad?" I wondered nervously.

Dr. Murray smiled, showing off nearly perfect teeth, and said, "No. I bet you'll be a better patient than I was."

But first, I had to make a good impression. This entailed getting impressions made of my teeth. I settled into a chair and opened wide as Dr. Murray gently inserted a pair of lip retractors into my big mouth. Then he stuck a mirror in there and began taking pictures. The inside of my mouth resembled the Grand Canyon with molars. I was going to suggest that the photos be sold as postcards, but I couldn't talk. For this outstanding achievement, Dr. Murray deserved to win the Nobel Prize.

After the photo shoot, Dr. Murray took out the lip retractors and inserted some waxy matter so I could make a wax bite. He then asked if I was having a gag reflex. I was going to say that my reflex is always to pull a gag when Dr. Murray said, "Last week, an eight-year-old boy threw up on me." As a good patient, I decided not to bring the matter up.

Now it was time for my impressions. Dr. Murray handed me a bib and some napkins. "You are going to drool," he assured me.

"There's no drool like an old drool," I said, at which point Dr. Murray shut me up by putting some seaweed-based material into my mouth, first on the top, then on the bottom. The stuff was like Play-Doh, only not as tasty.

"Don't bite down," Dr. Murray warned, "or you won't be able to open your mouth again." I think he was trying to use reverse psychology.

When it was over, Dr. Murray said that my case would be reviewed by the staff, including Dr. Richard Faber, director of postgraduate orthodontics at Stony Brook, to determine what kind of braces I would need.

A few weeks later, after the review, it was determined that I had fallen arches. This would have been bad enough if they were in my feet, or, even worse, if they fell while I was eating at McDonald's. But these arches were in my mouth.

Actually, my right maxillary arch was the site of the problem. The good news was that I qualified for invisible braces. The bad news was that first I would have to wear regular braces in my arch to straighten my teeth on that side and prepare them, and the rest of my mouth, for Invisalign.

Before anything could happen, however, I had to see Dr. Eugene Oh, an ace periodontist who gave me a series of "deep cleanings" that entailed freezing my face so I couldn't talk for most of the day. My family and friends were grateful.

Then I made an appointment with Janet Argentieri, a very nice orthodontic coordinator. "You'll see Dr. Murray next Wednesday at ten a.m.," she said with a bright smile.

At the scheduled time, I was sitting in a reclining chair as Dr. Murray and certified orthodontic assistant Celeste DeGeorge peered into my mouth. I decided to get braces with ceramic brackets instead of the conventional metal ones, not just because they were more aesthetic, but because they matched the cookware at home.

Dr. Murray said the invisible braces would be applied after these braces did their job, which was to push back the tightly packed teeth in the upper right side of my mouth so there would be room for my lateral incisor to be rotated to its original position. The invisible braces would then be applied to both my top and bottom teeth. When the treatment was over, Dr. Murray promised, I'd have the smile of a Hollywood star. I assumed he wasn't referring to Freddy Krueger.

"For now," Dr. Murray said, "we're working on the right buccal segment of the maxillary arch to distalize that area and correct the Class Two malocclusion."

"You took the words right out of my mouth," I replied.

What Dr. Murray put into my mouth was a track resembling a stretch of the Long Island Rail Road. It was a construction project that, I was relieved to find out, would not involve either jackhammers or dynamite.

"But we will have to use a blowtorch," Dr. Murray announced, adding that the flame would be applied to a wire not already in my mouth.

"You have very shiny teeth!" Celeste exclaimed. "What do you use on them?"

"Turtle Wax," I told her.

The procedure lasted less than an hour. It didn't hurt at all, even without Novocaine, and the braces, which began on my second molar, were mostly hidden by my cheek. I couldn't chew gum (especially while walking) and I had to avoid such hard or sticky foods as peanut brittle, caramel, and pizza crust. But I could still eat Chicken McNuggets to my heart's content. And I didn't have to worry about fallen arches.

Still, when I thought of history's classic constructions—the Great Pyramid of Giza, the Hanging Gardens of Babylon, the Green Monster at Fenway Park—I naturally thought of the Seven Wonders of the World. But there was another one that was so impressive, so outstanding, so absolutely fantastic that it should have been added to the list—my braces, which might have been called the Great Project of Geezer.

During a subsequent office visit, Dr. Murray drew up a blueprint of his work and explained it in layman's terms so even I could understand it.

"The lateral incisor is severely rotated," he said. It sounded like one of the tires on my car. At least he didn't call it a snaggletooth. Then I would have been like Snaggletooth, also known as Snagglepuss, the cartoon mountain lion ("Heavens to Murgatroyd!") on the old Yogi Bear TV show.

"The whole right side has moved forward," Dr. Murray continued. "This mesial shift is common in adults."

To straighten out this mess, Dr. Murray embarked on an engineering job involving screws, springs, wires, brackets, and anchor pins. It was like a suspension bridge. The only thing missing was a toll booth.

When Dr. Murray showed me his drawing, which resembled plans for a housing development, he said, "I put braces on the upper right teeth from the second molar to the canine. Then I put a TAD, also called a temporary anchorage device, between the premolars, and I distalized the second molar. The pin stabilizes the second molar and the first premolar. I retracted the first molar off the second molar and pushed the second molar back off the first premolar."

It all made perfect sense. The only glitch came when the pin, which was inserted in the outside of my gums, loosened due to hard brushing and wasn't strong enough to anchor the wire pulling my teeth backward. So Dr. Murray ingeniously put another TAD in my palatal mucosa on the inside. It worked like a charm.

A few months later, it was time for my first tray of invisible braces, which were applied only to my bottom teeth because I still had the regular braces on top. Unfortunately, as I snapped on the invisible braces, the crooked tooth on the bottom broke, so I had to go to my regular dentist, Dr. Salvatore Trentalancia, who has a practice in Stamford, to get the tooth bonded, James bonded.

"He did a fantastic job," Dr. Murray said of Dr. T, who goes by that nickname because it is tough to say "Trentalancia" while your mouth is open.

During my final visit with Dr. Murray, who was about to graduate and had landed a job with a practice north of Boston, he said he had discussed my case with a class of dental students.

"It was very interesting to them," he said, adding that I had been "a very good patient" who had "taken our torture pretty well."

It was hardly torture, but it was hardly over, either, because Dr. Murray left me in the capable hands of Dr. Michael Sheinis, a second-year resident who said, "I've heard a lot about you."

Dr. Sheinis, a brave man to be taking my case, would soon remove the traditional braces from my right upper teeth and replace them with Invisalign to match the invisible braces on the bottom. Both sets would cover all my teeth.

But first, the good doctor had to put cement in my mouth. Not blocks, which would have been appropriate because I'm a blockhead, but small attachments on a few of my teeth so the clear plastic braces could be snapped into place. At mealtime, I could pop out the upper and lower trays, stuff my face, brush my teeth, and put the braces back in. No one could see them. Only my orthodontist knew for sure.

"I won't tell anyone," promised Dr. Sheinis, who used a composite gun to apply the attachments. It looked like a cross between a caulker ("No, I didn't get it at Home Depot," he said) and the phaser Captain Kirk used on "Star Trek" ("Going where lots of other orthodontists have gone before," the doctor added).

On my next visit, Dr. Sheinis announced, "I have to do a little stripping."

"Keep your shirt on, doc," I urged.

"Not me," he replied reassuringly. "Your teeth. I have to strip some of the bottom ones so the invisible braces can move them more easily."

To do so, Dr. Sheinis used interproximal strips, which are essentially pieces of sandpaper floss. The idea was to slenderize the aforementioned teeth so the crooked one on the bottom could be pushed back into line with the others.

The stripping was done over three visits. "It keeps the shape of your teeth, but it narrows them a bit," explained Dr. Sheinis, who had braces—metal, not invisible—when he was ten.

"My dad's an orthodontist," he said. "He put every appliance in my mouth. I even had the headgear with the strap that comes out of your face. I had the lip bumper, too."

The only good part, Dr. Sheinis said, was that he got to pick which color elastic bands were used on his braces. "I always chose colors to match my favorite sports teams," the native Floridian said, referring to the Miami Dolphins (aqua and orange) and the Miami Heat (red and black).

His teeth were perfectly straight. "The braces worked," he said, noting that mine would, too.

But the job wouldn't be finished before Dr. Sheinis left. He, like Dr. Murray before him, was graduating. On my farewell visit with Dr. Sheinis, I met his successor, Dr. Stephanie Shinmachi, a second-year student. She was my third—and final—orthodontist at Stony Brook.

"You were great," Dr. Sheinis told me. "You showed up to your appointments, you did what you were told, and you have good hygiene."

"You mean some patients don't brush their teeth?" I asked.

"Sometimes their breath is so bad," Dr. Sheinis replied, "we have to put Vicks VapoRub under our noses."

"Or wear double masks," added Dr. Shinmachi.

Unlike Drs. Murray and Sheinis, she is the first person in her family to go into dentistry.

"I kind of fell into it," said Dr. Shinmachi, who grew up in Stony Brook. "I just like teeth."

Hers are flawless thanks to the braces (regular, not invisible) she wore as a kid.

"I'll see you in six weeks," Dr. Shinmachi said.

"I usually come back every four weeks," I noted.

"I know," she responded. "But I'll be in the Dominican Republic for my destination wedding."

"Cheers!" I said.

A month and a half later, Dr. Shinmachi sat me in the chair and told me about the fabulous time she, her husband, and their wedding party had in the Dominican Republic, adding that they had a ceremony on Long Island, too.

I told her about Lauren and Guillaume's wedding in France and the ceremony they later had on Long Island.

"Destination weddings are a big thing now," said Dr. Shinmachi, whose husband also is an orthodontist.

My appointments with Dr. Shinmachi continued for a few months, during which she used elastic bands to pull my top front teeth forward. She also put dimples in the upper Invisalign tray to help complete the rotation of my lateral incisor.

"And don't forget to use the chewy," she said, referring to the little rubber ring I had to bite down on for a few minutes each time I put my trays back in.

Finally, a little more than five years after my first appointment at Stony Brook, my orthodontic adventure was over. My teeth looked great, nice and straight, just as I hoped they would.

"You've been a terrific patient," said Dr. Richard Faber, head of the postgraduate program. "You're very cooperative and have a positive attitude. It's been a pleasure to have you."

The feeling was mutual. My experience, which cost about $5,000, most of which was covered by insurance, couldn't have been better. Drs. Murray, Sheinis, and Shinmachi were wonderful. So were Dr. Faber and his son, Dr. Zack Faber. Drs. Jonathan Fisk and Hechang Huang were wonderful, too, as were Janet, Judy, Celeste, Grace, and everyone else at the Dental Care Center.

I may not be on my way to Hollywood, but at least I have a much better smile. Now all I have to do is remember to keep my foot out of my mouth.

"Paste Makes Waste"

I have been a husband long enough to know that there is one marital problem that can't be brushed off. I refer, of course, to the toothpaste cap.

If there is one reason why many marriages go down the tubes, it's because either the husband or the wife doesn't put the cap back on the toothpaste. In our house, that person would be Sue.

Sue is perfect in every way except one: She either can't or won't secure the top of the toothpaste tube. In the early days of our marriage, all toothpaste tubes came with screw-on caps. The idea seemed simple enough except that Sue would never screw on the cap all the way. When I picked up the toothpaste, the cap would invariably fall off and land in the sink, on the floor, or, God forbid, in the toilet. (That's what I got for being a man who is genetically incapable of putting the toilet seat down.)

Apparently, this was not a problem unique to the Zezima household because in recent years, toothpaste companies have designed tubes with attached caps that can be lifted and snapped

---

back into place so they won't, despite the best sabotage efforts of certain spouses, fall in the toilet.

Unfortunately, the technology is flawed because toothpaste can build up on the opening of the tube and harden into a substance remarkably like Spackle, thus preventing the cap from being snapped closed. To complicate matters, those same certain spouses often put the tube on the vanity face down, creating a gummy mess.

But one day I beheld a scientific breakthrough that could save millions of marriages, at least among people who brush their teeth regularly. Sue came home with a tube of Colgate Luminous, which had an attached cap that was different from the others in that it was larger and looked more like a hood, meaning it could still be closed if toothpaste had built up on the tube. And that couldn't happen anyway because there was an X-shaped slitted opening in the tube that prevented such a buildup.

For the record, this is not an endorsement of Colgate because: (a) the company isn't paying me and (b) an endorsement from me is usually the kiss of death. But I was so impressed by the ingenious design, which made it impossible even for Sue to make a mess of the toothpaste, that I decided to track down the inventor.

His name is Joe Norris, a packaging development engineer from Cumming, Georgia, who holds United States Design Patent No. US D531,504 S. In layman's terms, he got it for inventing the spouse-proof toothpaste cap.

When I called Joe, I first spoke with his wife, Terri, who said, with no small amount of pride, that she may have been the inspiration for his invention.

"I used to complain about the toothpaste," she explained. "There was always a mess. He brought home all different tubes he was working on, but this was the only one that was clean. I don't know if he did it because of me, but I was very happy when he came out with it."

Joe began his career at Coca-Cola, where he designed the plastic soft drink can. He worked for Colgate for fourteen years before going back to Coke. He started working on his toothpaste cap and slitted tube opening with John Crawford, Scott Walsh, and Peter Stagl. Three years later, Joe was awarded the patent.

"I gave Colgate my 'Field of Dreams' speech: Let me build it and they will come," Joe said, adding that he was responding to consumer complaints. "You're not the only one who had a toothpaste problem," he assured me.

"This must be your greatest triumph," I said. "You deserve to win the Nobel Prize."

"I wouldn't go that far," Joe said modestly, "but I do remember my kids' friends saying, 'Wow!' when I brought it home. And my wife liked it."

Sue likes it, too, although I think she's a little disappointed because she can't sabotage my toothpaste anymore. That's a feather in Joe Norris's cap.

Chapter 13

*A tough economy is tough on empty nesters, especially
when you have to deal with the bank and factor in the cost
of the gas it takes to go to work so you can afford
to stay in the house.*

"Banks for Nothing"

Jamie Dimon
President and CEO
JPMorgan Chase
270 Park Ave.
New York, N.Y. 10017

Dear Mr. Dimon:

I'm Jerry Zezima. The name probably doesn't mean much to you (it doesn't mean much to me, either, although it is of great interest to my creditors), but I am a Chase customer who, like you, has been victimized by the bad housing market.

I am writing to tell you that I sympathize with your recent decision to sell your Chicago mansion for only $6.95 million, which is about half the original asking price of $13.5 million. My wife, Sue, and I had been trying to refinance our house, which is nice but certainly no mansion, and just found out that we have been denied by your bank.

It all started when we went to our local Chase branch and saw a very nice loan officer named Ernie. Let me say from the outset that you should give Ernie a raise. I'd give him one myself, but because of the denial, I don't have the extra cash. Then again, you know the feeling.

So we began the Application From Hell. Little did Sue and I know that the process would take almost six months. I am now convinced that the full name of your bank is Wild Goose Chase.

We had to produce enough paperwork to wipe out the Amazon rainforest, the Maine North Woods, and all the trees in our yard. Scientists may well blame Chase for climate change.

Practically every day I had to drop off copies of pay stubs, insurance forms, bank statements, income tax returns, and so much other stuff I could barely carry it all. I'm surprised I wasn't required to bring my high school transcript, which would have shown that I am so bad at math, I could get a job as an underwriter.

For the record, your underwriters not only are underhanded and overrated but also sadistic. They kept asking for personal information (I wear size 34 boxer shorts, by the way) but were never satisfied. So I had to produce even more evidence that Sue and I still live in our house, still have jobs, and, perhaps most important, are still alive.

It got to the point where I was spending more time with Ernie than I was with Sue. People were starting to talk.

Then we had to shell out $400 for a house appraisal. It turned out that our house was acceptable but we weren't. So our application was denied.

I don't know what you are going to do about the hit you took on the sale of your Chicago house, but if you are thinking of recouping the money by refinancing your home in Westchester County, I have two words of advice: Forget it!

Take it from me, Mr. Dimon: It will be the worst experience of your life.

I am telling you all this because I know you're not a bad guy. In fact, The New York Times called you "America's least hated banker." You should put that on your business card.

Since you live fairly close to our place on Long Island, Sue and I would like to invite you over to the house, which I am sure you will like. You may even wonder why we weren't able to refinance it.

In the meantime, Mr. Dimon, good luck. If you need to borrow a few bucks until payday, I'd be happy to help. And at a low interest rate. After all, in these tough times, we homeowners have to stick together.

Sincerely,
Jerry Zezima

"The Loan Arranger"

Ever since Sue and I were rejected for a home refinancing loan by our bank, which actually owns the house but kindly allows us to pay the mortgage, I have been wondering what we did wrong. The answer, I now realize, is that I didn't rob the bank.

I will say for the record that I would never resort to bank robbery. And our loan officer, Ernie, who has been in the banking business for about thirty years, is so ethical and honest that I call him the Loan Arranger. He's not a masked man, but he is a straight shooter. And a good guy.

"Times are tough," Ernie said when I went back to case the joint—or, rather, to pay the mortgage. "And people are frustrated."

A classic example, Ernie recalled, was the guy who had been put through the wringer by the underwriters, who kept asking him for pay stubs, insurance forms, bank statements, everything but his birth certificate.

"Nothing he provided was good enough to get his refinancing application approved, so they kept asking for more," Ernie said. "The guy got so angry that when the underwriters demanded to see where he kept his money, he took a picture of a stainless steel box with an arrow pointing to it. He said, 'The money is in the box.' I was hysterical. But the underwriters weren't amused. They said, 'Open the box and give us pictures of George Washington.' The guy didn't get the loan."

It's stuff like this, Ernie said, that causes people to try to outwit underwriters—not a very difficult task, he and I agreed, because they seem pretty witless.

"They're stupid. They have no common sense," said Ernie, who remembered the guy who pooled his resources by hiding his pool.

"He had a built-in swimming pool that he didn't have a certificate of occupancy for," Ernie said. "The guy took the ladders out of his pool, put plywood over the whole thing, threw dirt and grass seed over it, and roped it off. He told the appraiser not to walk on that area because it was freshly seeded. The appraiser never suspected and the guy was approved. He got away with it."

Then there was the guy who got approved by not having an open-door policy.

"He had converted the garage to a living space that he didn't have a certificate of occupancy for," Ernie recalled. "He took the facade off the front of the house and put two garage doors up. They didn't work, so you couldn't open them, but the appraiser didn't know because he never checked. Most appraisers don't bother to go into the garage. This guy got away with it, too."

So did the guy who used pull to get approved.

"He had a huge deck on the back of his house that he didn't have a permit for," Ernie said. "He also had a huge tree by the deck, so he devised a pulley system on the tree to pull up the appraiser, who went along with it. The appraiser took pictures of the back of the house from above that never showed the deck."

Of course, some plans backfire, which is what happened to a guy who tried to doctor his W2 form but put down the wrong address for a company he said he worked for but didn't.

"He wasn't that sharp," said Ernie, adding that he would never go along with such chicanery. "My reputation is involved," he said.

Still, Ernie said, banks have been robbing people for so long that some people have decided to use pens and ingenuity instead of guns and bravado to rob banks.

"It'll keep happening," Ernie promised. "You can bank on it."

"Horsepower"

A horse is a horse, of course, of course, unless you buy one to replace your car, of course. So it should come as no surprise that I couldn't get the "Mister Ed" theme song out of my head when I came up with the solution to America's gas crisis.

I am not suggesting that we stop eating baked beans, although that might help. Instead, I think we should all ditch our fuel-guzzling automobiles and, as the old saying goes, get a horse.

That's what I did when I got in my SUV and drove all the way out to Montauk, New York, home of Deep Hollow Ranch, which not only is billed as "America's Oldest Cattle Ranch (est. 1658)," but also is eastern Long Island's only horse dealership.

"What make and model are you looking for?" asked Rusty Leaver, who runs Deep Hollow Ranch and is the firm's top salesman.

"Nothing fancy," I said. "Something that gets good mileage and doesn't cost a lot to run."

Rusty sat me down to crunch numbers.

"Would you like to buy or lease?" he asked.

"What's the better deal?" I replied.

"Leasing is an option," Rusty said, "but it's more economical to buy. You can get a good horse—not a new model and not with a full warranty, but something very reliable—for $2,000 to $3,000."

I was almost sold right there because a good car costs ten times that much. I was even more enthusiastic when Rusty told me that it costs only $150 a month to feed a horse.

"I spend about $80 a week on gas," I said.

"So you'd be cutting your fuel outlay by more than half," Rusty pointed out.

I could save even more, Rusty said, if I didn't board my horse, which costs about $500 a month.

"I have a garage, so the horse could stay in there," I said. "Or it could stay in the backyard. In fact, the horse could cut my grass."

"That way," Rusty said, "you'd save on gas for your power mower."

I could also save on service costs because the annual veterinary bill for a horse is about $500. With tune-ups, inspections, and other regular maintenance, I spend more than that on my car.

Insurance is another saving. According to Rusty, it costs only $200 a year to insure a horse. Insurance on my car is more than $1,500 annually.

True, it costs about $50 a month (or $600 a year) to shoe a horse, which is more than I pay for tires, but I'd still be way ahead if I made the switch.

As for going to work, a horse is much slower than a car, even though, of course, it has more horsepower. But a commuter can make the ride easier, Rusty said, by getting a carriage. "Here," he added, "is where the Amish are way ahead of us."

Rusty's sales pitch was great, but I wanted to go out for a test drive, so I went to the showroom to look over the inventory. Rusty's wife, Diane, whose family has owned Deep Hollow Ranch for six generations, said I could take Junior for a spin.

Junior, "a pre-owned vehicle with a lot of mileage," according to Diane, is fifteen years old, but he is in "excellent condition." Then she added, "And he starts right up."

Junior was everything a middle-age guy could want: a convertible with bucket seating and, with a mere flick of the reins, power steering. Granted, he couldn't go from zero to sixty in three seconds, but he offered a smooth, comfortable ride. A driver's-side hair bag, which makes use of his mane in case of a collision, is standard equipment.

Accompanying me on the test drive was trail guide Kalila Fahey, fourteen, who was riding Zip, eight, one of about one hundred and twenty horses at Deep Hollow Ranch. Kalila, who doesn't have her driver's license yet, said, "You don't need a license to ride a horse."

Half an hour later, we were back in the showroom.

"How did you like Junior?" Diane asked.

"I'll take him," I said.

Now all I have to do is go to the bank for a horse loan.

"They Mean Business"

Ever since the economy turned so sour that a lemon would seem sweet by comparison, I have wondered if there are any entrepreneurs out there with a bold business model that can help get the country back on its feet.

I am happy to report that I recently found two of them. They are Sydney Lippman and Isabella Nuzzo, co-owners of Syd and Izzy's Lemonade Stand, a budding Fortune 500 corporation headquartered in one of the nation's top corporate headquarters, my hometown of Stamford.

I met them on Scofieldtown Road, where Sydney and Isabella, both ten years old and fifth-graders at Northeast Elementary School, had set up shop. In a brilliant advertising ploy designed to attract customers quickly, the girls were shouting and waving their arms as I drove down the street.

As a father who remembers when Katie and Lauren sold lemonade and made more money than I had in my wallet at the time, mainly because the money in my wallet went to buy their lemonade, I turned around and parked near the stand.

"You're our first customer!" Isabella chirped.

It felt good to get in on the ground floor—or at least the ground, since that's where the stand was situated—of such a promising enterprise.

The girls' corporate slogan, "When life gives you lemons, make lemonade," was handsomely hand-lettered on the cardboard sign attached to the front of the stand.

"Did you actually make this lemonade?" I asked the two young entrepreneurs, who also had written "Secret recipe!" on a corner of the sign.

"Yes," Sydney assured me.

The tycoons explained that they had squeezed the juice of several lemons into water but that it was taking too much time, so they combined their lemonade with a store-bought brand to come up with their now-not-so-secret (sorry, girls) recipe.

It was uniquely delicious. And worth every penny of the fifty cents they charged per cup.

"We were going to charge $2," Sydney said, "but we thought it would be unfair to overcharge people, so we decided to charge fifty cents."

If you have a fair price, customers will buy more of your product and you will end up making more money, the girls noted.

I was impressed, not only with their business acumen, but with their approach to customer service.

"In business, you don't want to be too grumpy to your customers," Isabella said. "Always smile," she added with, of course, a smile.

At this moment, a woman and her two young daughters came along and bought three cups of Syd and Izzy's lemonade.

"This is very good!" the woman exclaimed. Her daughters agreed.

"If you have a quality product," Sydney confided after they left, "people will buy it."

"Business leaders and politicians could learn a lot from you girls," I said. "If they followed your example of combining quality with fair pricing and good customer service, the economy would rebound."

"We would be happy to give them tips," said Isabella, who is thinking of selling the bracelets she has made out of soda can pop-top rings. She also has a line of colorful duct tape products, including a pocketbook and a wallet.

"She's very entrepreneurial," said Isabella's mom, Gerri Nuzzo, whose older daughter, Ariana, fourteen, also is creative and would be part of the corporate team.

When I called back later in the afternoon, Gerri reported that Syd and Izzy's Lemonade Stand had grossed $10 in two and a half hours, pretty good considering that Scofieldtown is not a heavily traveled road.

"They did all right," Gerri said.

Sydney's dad, Craig Lippman, concurred when I spoke with him by phone a couple of days later.

"I'm delighted that my daughter understands the supply-and-demand curve," said Craig, who works in financial markets for Thomson Reuters. "I'll go back and cut prices if it will increase business." He paused and added: "I could learn a lot from these girls. The whole country could."

Chapter 14

"Blowing Hot and Cold"

Most people who work in modern office buildings are convinced there is no such thing as climate control. I believe otherwise. Here's why: When it's 92 degrees outside, it's 52 inside. Add them up and divide by two and that's how you get an average temperature of 72 degrees.

Still, I have told Sue that I don't have to change my seasonal wardrobe—put winter clothes away in the spring and take out summer ones, put summer clothes away in the fall and take out winter ones—because you never know what the temperature is going to be in the office.

Instead, I suggest that you take a suitcase to work every day so you can change clothes if it's either too hot or too cold.

To warm up to the subject, I spoke with a cool guy, Steve Zimmerman, director of engineering services in the building where I work.

"We do get our fair share of complaints about the temperature," said Steve, who was wearing a long-sleeve shirt and a tie (and, of course, pants) even though it was a hot day.

"Actually, I think it's pretty comfortable in here today," I said, dressed in a sweatshirt (it was "casual Friday," even if Steve wasn't observing it) with a T-shirt underneath and a pair of jeans. I had also brought a windbreaker in case the wind in the office broke the record for the low temperature on that date. (Office conditions are not monitored by the National Weather Service, but they should be.)

Regulating the temperature in the building, which is half a million square feet, is "a big challenge," Steve said, adding: "We have three air compressors on the roof. And we have chillers in the basement. They have a series of pipes that blow air over the coils. There's a lot of wear and tear on the equipment. We try to keep it comfortable, but you can't please everybody. Some people say they're too hot; others say they're freezing. It's a constant battle."

It's also a battle at home, said Steve, who doesn't have central air-conditioning.

"I recently put air conditioners in the windows," he said.

"I put one in the bedroom because it gets too hot up there," I said.

"My wife is always hot," said Steve. "She'll open the window in February. I'll have five blankets on and she'll be on top of the sheet."

"Have you told her that you shouldn't have to change your seasonal wardrobe?" I asked.

"If I had the space I would," said Steve, adding that he boxes his clothes for the appropriate season.

"But you're wearing a shirt and tie today," I noted.

"I have to dress professionally no matter what the temperature is," Steve explained.

In the summer, the temperature in the office can be so cold that the place feels like a meat locker.

"Maybe," I suggested, "we can hang sides of beef in here and use them as punching bags, like Sylvester Stallone did in the first 'Rocky' movie. It would be a good way to keep in shape."

"It might also make somebody want to punch you," Steve said.

"Good point," I replied.

In the winter, the temperature in the office can be so hot that the place feels like a sauna.

"Maybe," I suggested, "we can make it like a real sauna on casual Fridays and wear towels."

"If yours fell off, you might not have a job anymore," Steve said.

"Another good point," I replied.

I gained new respect for Steve and all the other people who, through broiling heat and bone-chilling cold, try to keep the temperature comfortable in office buildings across the land.

Now, if you will excuse me, I have to pack a suitcase for work.

"Bad Connections"

If Alexander Graham Bell were still alive—in which case I would demand reimbursement for all of the phone bills Katie and Lauren racked up when they were living at home—he would call his assistant, Thomas Watson, to say, "Watson, come here, I need you to show me how to operate this stupid new telephone system."

But instead of talking with Watson, Bell would hear this recording: "I'm sorry, your call cannot be completed as dialed. Please check the number and try again."

So Bell would actually have to take a class to learn how to use his own invention.

That's what I had to do when we got new phones at work.

"I haven't heard this much swearing in the seven years I've been here," said Tommy, a contractor who was taking away the old phones, which were practically tin cans connected by strings compared to the new ones.

I wanted to say some bad words myself—directly into the phone, if possible—when I went to my training class and had to wait twenty minutes because the previous class, which was supposed to be forty-five minutes, lasted more than an hour.

The people who walked out seemed dazed and confused. Nigel, the instructor, who had been giving classes all day, seemed tired. "Sorry," he said as half a dozen of us sat down in front of the new phones, "but my voice is a little scratchy."

"Sounds like a bad connection," I noted.

Nigel, a very nice guy, smiled wearily. Then he explained that we would be working on a system called Cisco Unified IP Phone 7942G, as opposed to another system called Cisco Unified IP Phone 7962G.

"If the two systems got together," I asked, "would they have a Cisco kid?" Then I sang a line from my own version of the War song: "Cisco kid's not a friend of mine."

As punishment, the phone in front of me refused to work.

"Press the help button," Nigel said.

It was one of sixteen buttons on the phone, which also had a screen on which I could not, regrettably, watch something intellectual, like baseball or the Three Stooges.

Other buttons included the footstand button (what, no handstand button?) and the mute button (for mimes, I guess). As if to reciprocate, the phone was pressing my buttons.

"The soft keys are where the action is," Nigel said.

I pressed a soft key, the only thing about the phone that wasn't hard, and heard a woman's disembodied voice say, "Invalid entry." I pressed another key. She said it again.

"Shut up!" I shouted.

"You have to speak into the phone," said Nigel, who then had us practice calling each other. Daria, who sat next to me, called my number. I picked up the receiver and said, "I'm sorry, your call cannot be completed as dialed. Please check the number and try again."

The rest of the class went pretty smoothly, thanks to Nigel's patience and good humor. I wish I could say the same for the phones, which have been giving everybody trouble.

Fortunately, I didn't have any trouble recording my voice mail greeting: "Hi, this is Jerry Zezima. I'm either away from my desk or at my desk but fast asleep. Please leave a message and I'll get back to you."

Don't bet on it. I am now in Alexander Graham Hell. Watson, come here, I need you.

"iBought a New Phone"

With apologies to Gilbert and Sullivan, who are dead and can't sue me, I'm the very model of the modern middle-age man. Except, unfortunately, when it comes to technology.

Until recently, I didn't have an iPhone, an iPad, an iPod, or iTunes, although I did have iTeeth.

At the urging of Sue, who got into the twenty-first century when it actually started, I exchanged my dumbphone for a smartphone.

And it cost me only ninety-nine cents.

"What would you like your phone to do?" asked Syed, a nice and knowledgeable retail sales consultant at the AT&T store.

"I'd like it to pick the winning Powerball numbers," I responded.

"If I could find a phone like that," Syed said, "I wouldn't be working here."

"My old phone is no help," I said, showing Syed the ancient Samsung I had been using—or trying to use—for the past several years.

"He doesn't even know how to retrieve messages," Sue told Syed.

"It doesn't matter," I said in my own defense. "Nobody wants to talk with me anyway."

Then I explained that my original cellphone, which the Samsung replaced, came with a one-hundred-thirty-four-page user guide.

"My daughters had to program it for me," I said. "It used to be that all you had to know about the telephone was that you said 'hello' when you picked it up and 'goodbye' when you put it down."

"Things have changed," Syed said.

"Do you know when telephone technology was at its peak?" I asked him.

"When?" Syed wondered.

"The day Alexander Graham Bell invented it," I said. "It's been all downhill from there. Now the industry is defined by this phrase: 'Can you hear me now?' Even the phone makers don't expect the stupid thing to work."

Sue helpfully pointed out that I was, as usual, wrong.

"The phone works fine if you're standing in the right place," she said.

I used my phone to call hers. It didn't ring.

"See what I mean?" I said. "I'm standing right next to you!"

It was the mission of Syed, a twenty-two-year-old college student who grew up with technology, to modernize me, a fifty-eight-year-old geezer who not only hasn't grown up but remembers when high-tech was an electric typewriter.

"Are you looking for an iPhone?" Syed asked.

"iGuess," I replied.

"I would recommend the iPhone 4," he said.

"What happened to the first three?" I inquired. "Didn't they work, either?"

"They got upgraded," said Syed. "That's what I am going to do with you."

"So I'll be the iJerry 4?" I said. "It sounds like a rock group."

Sue looked at me like I had rocks in my head.

Syed was too kind to agree, so he said, "I think I can help you. I have nothing better to do."

When I told Syed that he has an excellent sense of humor, he replied, "I'm a hoot. The saddest thing about me is that I'm not around myself when I tell jokes."

It's a good thing he was around the store when Sue and I came in because he explained in simple terms what the iPhone offered, including a feature that lets me write drivel like this without having to get on a computer. Or an electric typewriter.

"It's perfect for your lifestyle," Syed said.

"I really don't have a life," I explained.

"That means you'll have more time to enjoy it," he said.

"Now you can retrieve messages," Sue said.

"Even though nobody wants to talk with you," Syed chimed in.

The phone, which ordinarily costs $549, was only ninety-nine cents with my contract.

"I appreciate the savings," I said, "but I'd still like to win Powerball."

"Sorry," Syed told me. "That's the one thing your new phone can't do."

"Get the Picture?"

If there is one thing I have found out from being on Facebook—aside from the incredible fact that I have more friends than the guy who founded it—it's that a picture is indeed worth a thousand words.

I made this fascinating discovery when I posted a new profile photo of myself. I had it taken because my old photo was being used in bars all across this great land by drunken dart players. This just added to the holes in my head.

So I opted for an updated profile picture. I figured it was about time. Besides, practically everybody in the United States is on Facebook. My mother was on it before I was. And all of these people are constantly changing their profile photos or posting new shots of themselves. Sometimes the pictures are not exactly flattering.

Therein lay my dilemma: Would my new photo actually look like me? Would my Facebook friends mistake me for the Phantom of the Opera? Would people start sending Sue condolence cards?

Fortunately, I had the good sense to ask a colleague named Andreas, a talented photographer and a very patient guy, to shoot me. After the trouble I put him through, he probably wanted to.

But the result was worth it. The new photo, I must say with all due modesty, will not scare small children.

"It's nice," said Martha, who works at a nearby Apple store. I went there because I am so technologically inept that I needed a lesson in how to post my photo in places other than the post office.

The procedure is so astonishingly simple that even a kindergartner could do it. Unfortunately, I don't know any kindergartners, so I took a computer lesson.

Along with my original profile shot, photos of me have been posted, or "tagged," by other people. This was the first time I attempted to do it myself.

The reaction has been very gratifying.

Wendy wrote: "You don't age. Not fair."

My response: "I'm shockingly immature, Wendy. It makes me seem younger."

Bozena wrote: "Nice shot, Jerry. Nice jacket, too."

My response: "Thanks, Bozena. I had to give the jacket back after the photo shoot. I kept the pants."

Leland wrote: "What a great picture. That should be your 'If I ever get kidnapped, use this picture' picture."

My response: "If anybody kidnapped me, Leland, it would turn into 'The Ransom of Red Chief.'"

This got me thinking: I wonder if Facebook founder Mark Zuckerberg would like my new profile photo?

Except for money, power, and influence, I have a lot in common with Zuckerberg because, of course, our last names begin with Z.

So I went to his Facebook page. There was Mark, in all his geeky glory, grinning goofily in a black-and-white photo.

I wanted to friend him, and ask what he thinks of my new profile picture, but I couldn't. All I could do was click on "Like" and read his postings.

Incredibly, and a little sadly, the genius behind Facebook has no friends.

Don't worry, Mark. I'll be your friend. But first, get a new profile picture.

"Down to a Science"

You don't have to be a rocket scientist to write a newspaper column, but sometimes it helps to be a nuclear physicist.

Aside from realizing that I'm not smart enough to be either, which is why I write a newspaper column, that's the lesson I learned recently after Sue and I went on a tour of Brookhaven National Laboratory in Upton, New York.

We were among the approximately eighteen hundred people who saw the lab that day as part of Brookhaven's Sunday Summer Tours. The program allows the public to view virtually every major part of the sprawling laboratory, which is operated in conjunction with the U.S. Department of Energy and has won seven Nobel Prizes.

Our group was welcomed by nuclear physicist Phil Pile, who said, "The world's most perfect liquid was discovered here."

"Wow!" I whispered to Sue. "They're going to serve beer."

No such luck. Phil was referring to a type of matter thought to have existed microseconds after the Big Bang. This means, I guess, that it was microbrewed.

The Big Bang is the prevailing cosmological theory of how the universe was created and is not to be confused with the Big Band, from which popular music was created.

Brookhaven is famous for the Relativistic Heavy Ion Collider, aka RHIC, pronounced Rick, which makes the laboratory Rick's Place.

"Of all the lab joints in all the towns in all the world, you had to walk into ours," Phil didn't say to the group.

He did say, however, that RHIC, where the origin of the universe is studied, is the first machine capable of colliding ions as heavy as gold.

"Maybe I'll get some jewelry out of this," Sue suggested.

Phil said that accelerated particles in RHIC have been known to travel seven hundred million miles per hour, which is almost as fast as some drivers go on Interstate 95 or the Long Island Expressway.

Phil also talked about protons and neutrons, though he didn't mention morons, probably because he didn't want to embarrass me. But he didn't spare Albert Einstein (e=MC Hammer), who was shown in a photo riding a bicycle without a helmet. "Not very smart," Phil said.

Our group then got on a bus headed for STAR, one of two detectors we would see. STAR stands for Solenoidal Tracker At Relativistic. Xian Li, a brilliant doctorate student, told us how heavy ions are smashed together in a structure that looks like a huge roulette wheel.

Even more brilliant was a twelve-year-old girl named Mikaela Egbert, who showed me how to use my cellphone to take pictures.

Our next stop was the other detector, PHENIX, which stands for Pioneering High Energy Nuclear Interactions eXperiment. Aside from not being in Arizona, PHENIX also is where scientists collide heavy ions. Protons are collided in both detectors as well.

The last stop was the Tunnel, where an accelerator physicist named Mei Bai said the lab spends $600 million on parts.

"Do you go to Home Depot?" I inquired.

"When we need ladders," she responded.

Accelerator physicist Todd Satogata talked about the Brookhaven Graphite Research Reactor, or BGRR. "It's affectionately known as Booger," he said.

Our group was given a tour by my son-in-law Guillaume, also an accelerator physicist. He is even smarter than that twelve-year-old girl and will one day win the Nobel Prize. You read it here first.

"This is where the magic happens," said Guillaume, adding: "The person who asks the best question wins a T-shirt."

"Can you use E-ZPass in this tunnel?" I asked.

I didn't win the shirt.

But Guillaume gave a winning presentation, which included a detailed description of the 2.4-mile-long tunnel's two concentric rings, which are made up of 1,740 superconducting magnets. "They're not the kind you put on your refrigerator door," he said.

After the tour, Sue said, "This was like being with Bill Nye the Science Guy."

The whole day was fun and fascinating. The best thing I learned is that, when it comes to riding a bike without a helmet, Albert Einstein was no smarter than me.

Chapter 15

Occasionally an empty nester of the male persuasion has to go out by himself and do guy stuff, mainly because his wife, an empty nester of the female persuasion, is too smart— or scared—to go along.

"Have a Knife Day"

I am proud and slightly flummoxed to say that I have done some incredibly stupid things in my life, which is why I am not considered the sharpest knife in the drawer. And I proved it when I was a target for a knife thrower known as the Great Throwdini.

Throw, as he is called by his many friends and admirers in the impalement arts, is in the Guinness Book of World Records for being the world's fastest and most accurate knife thrower. He has received magic's highest honor, the coveted Merlin Award. He is the only artist to perform the Veiled Wheel of Death. And he has made many television appearances, including humorist Bill Geist's profile of him on "CBS News Sunday Morning." His slogan: "Throwetry in Motion."

Because Throw lives a knife's throw from my house, I arranged to pay him a visit and, for once, do something that wasn't pointless.

The first thing I noticed about Throw is that he wears glasses.

"I'm blind as a bat without them," he admitted.

I gulped. What was I getting myself into? Even more unnerving, what would be getting into me?

But Throw took great pains, so to speak, to put me at ease. His real name is the Rev. Dr. David R. Adamovich. He is a minister in a nondenominational Christian church.

"I've never had to give anyone last rites," he assured me.

He also has a doctorate in exercise physiology and for eighteen years was a college professor of electrocardiography.

"I didn't get into knife throwing until I was fifty," said Throw, who is sixty-four.

He is so good that he can throw ten knives in 3.9 seconds. Even more impressive is that he performs with a Target Girl who stands against a board or is attached to a spinning wheel while Throw throws knives that land within inches of her.

"It's fun," said Lynn Wheat, one of Throw's several Target Girls. Lynn, twenty-seven, who teaches theatrical carpentry on the college level, said she enjoys motorcycles and fast cars, adding: "I like to do crazy things."

One of them was being on the Wheel of Death for the "Sunday Morning" segment. As the wheel spun with Lynn attached to it, Throw threw the tools of his trade. When the wheel stopped, Lynn was closely surrounded by a chilling array of large, glistening knives.

"My mother saw it on TV," Lynn related. "Her only complaint was that I showed too much cleavage."

I wasn't showing anything except the tiniest hint of sheer panic as the three of us headed up to the attic, where I was about to make my debut—but not, thank God, my farewell—as a Target Boy.

"What advice would you give me?" I asked Lynn.

"Go with the flow," she answered.

"Of blood?" I stammered.

Lynn shook her head and smiled. She said I should enjoy the experience and have complete confidence in Throw.

"I do," she said. "And I'm still here."

She was still there after Throw stood her against a six-foot-high, four-foot-wide red wooden board and threw eight fourteen-inch knives around her in rapid succession from a distance of seven feet. Then she turned sideways and clenched a black cocktail straw between her teeth as one of Throw's sixteen-inch knives snapped off the spangled tip.

Next it was my turn to throw knives—but not at Lynn, who wisely had no confidence in me. Throw showed me how to hold a knife, cock my arm, and release the fearsome implement. My first one thudded off the board, but most of my subsequent throws stuck firmly in the wood.

"You're good," Throw said. "Now comes the real test."

I stood with my back to the board and looked straight at Throw. A strange sense of calm pervaded me. Thwap-thwap-thwap-thwap went the knives to my left; thwap-thwap-thwap-thwap to my right, the closest impaled three inches from my ear.

"You didn't flinch," Throw said. "You're an excellent Target Boy."

Just call me the Great Throwdummy.

"An Arrow Escape"

When I was a kid, I wanted to be like Robin Hood, except I wouldn't be caught dead in tights. But I did love the concept of using a bow and arrows to rob from the rich and give to the poor.

Now that I'm an adult with two kids I put through college and married off, I'd rob from the rich and keep the money myself.

To find out how, I went to Smith Point Archery in Patchogue, New York.

"We've had students ranging from four years old to ninety," said owner Jared Schneider. "I'm guessing you are somewhere in between."

"Physically I'm closer to the higher end," I responded, "but intellectually I'm in the opposite direction."

"Perfect," said Schneider, thirty-two, a former New York state archery champion who began shooting arrows when he was five.

"When I was five, I had those little rubber-tipped suction arrows," I told him.

"The arrows we have here are a little stronger than that," said Schneider, adding that archery has become very popular, not just because of the Olympics, but because of "The Hunger Games," the young-adult novel that was turned into a blockbuster movie.

"I haven't seen the film," I told Schneider, "but I've watched 'The Adventures of Robin Hood' about a dozen times."

"We have Robin Hood-style bows," said Schneider, referring to the traditional one-piece weapons, as opposed to high-tech compound bows.

Then he had one of his merry men show me how to use one.

Troy Kenny introduced himself by saying, "Never trust a guy with two first names."

I said, "Never trust a guy who has never tried archery."

"I bet you'll be shooting bull's-eyes in no time," said Kenny, forty-one, who has been an archer since he was twelve.

"Do you think I can be as good as William Tell and shoot an apple off someone's head?" I asked.

"I'm not going to volunteer," said Kenny, who presumably didn't want to look like Steve Martin with a fake arrow through his skull. "But I think you'll do all right. You can eat the apple when you get home."

He showed me the recurve bow and field-point arrows I would be using.

"Where do you buy your equipment?" I wondered. "Target?"

"No," he replied. "But we have plenty of targets here."

The one I would be shooting at was ten yards away. More advanced archers shoot at targets positioned at twice that distance.

Kenny handed me the bow and explained that the arrow, with the cock feather facing me, would rest on an anchor point, and that the arrow's notched end, or nock, would be fitted onto the nocking point of the bowstring.

I stood facing a wall and turned my body ninety degrees toward the target.

"Hold your left arm straight out," Kenny said, adding that I should put three fingers below the nock and pull back on the bowstring.

"Your form is very good," he said. "Take aim and slide your fingers off the string."

I shot an arrow in the air; where it landed was just not fair: I missed the target completely, though I did hit the large board on which it was mounted.

"Don't worry," Kenny said. "Try again."

My next shot hit the outermost ring of the target. The one after that was closer to the center. The one after that was even better.

Then, on my fifth shot: Bull's-eye!

"Great!" Kenny exclaimed. "Now all you need is a Robin Hood bull's-eye. That means your next shot has to split the first bull's-eye arrow."

My next shot wasn't even close. Neither were the six other arrows I shot before giving up.

"I'm no Robin Hood," I admitted.

"That's OK," Kenny said consolingly. "At least you don't have to wear tights."

"Batter Up!"

I don't like to brag about my athletic prowess, mainly because I don't have any, but I must say that I was a pretty good baseball player in my day. Unfortunately, that day was June 4, 1965, when I got a double in a Little League game. It was the highlight of an otherwise unremarkable career.

I never did realize my dream of making it to the big leagues and becoming the all-time home run champion. And now I know why: I didn't wear jasmine-scented wristbands.

They're better than steroids because they're safe, they're legal, and they don't have to be injected into your butt. And they were developed by my favorite mad scientist, Dr. Alan Hirsch, the founder and neurological director of the Smell & Taste Treatment and Research Foundation in Chicago.

In his latest study, "The Effects of Aroma of Jasmine on Major League Baseball Players," Hirsch worked with the Chicago White Sox before a regular-season game. Six players in a batting cage alternated sniffing regular cotton wristbands and those that smelled of jasmine.

"They were independently assessed regarding the mechanics of their swings, including trajectory, ball flight, bat speed, and bat swing zone," Hirsch said in the study. "Compared to the no-odor trials, jasmine significantly improved all batting parameters."

Seeing this as a chance to restart my baseball career, I called Hirsch to discuss strategy. But first I wanted to know why this Cubs fan chose to study his team's cross-town rivals.

"I'm not sure anything would work with the Cubs," said Hirsch, noting that they haven't won the World Series since 1908. "At least the White Sox have potential."

As for the study, Hirsch found that the scent of jasmine is relaxing, which helps calm players and improve hand-eye coordination.

"I didn't think they should come to bat wearing scented masks, so we used the wristbands," said Hirsch, adding that he doesn't believe the bands have been used in games. "I suppose a team could have jasmine air fresheners in the dugout. And I can see a player with the sniffles being put on the disabled list."

"I've been on the disabled list since Little League," I said. "Do you think a jasmine wristband could help me make it to the majors?"

"Maybe with the Cubs," said Hirsch, who mailed me a scented wristband.

Immediately after receiving it, I called Winner's Edge Sports Training, an indoor facility in Huntington Station, New York, and scheduled a session in the batting cage with instructor Chad Ross.

"Most of our students are eight or nine years old, so you definitely are the oldest one we've ever had," said Ross, twenty-seven, who has been playing baseball since he was four. He was a hitting instructor at Farmingdale State College and plays in an adult recreational league.

At first, Ross had me hit baseballs off a tee. Some of them went as far as three feet. Then he worked on my stance and the mechanics of my swing. After that, he pitched beach balls to me. I actually hit some.

Finally, the real test: Batting practice with baseballs tossed by Ross.

I put on a regular cotton wristband and sniffed it. Then I got in my stance and waited for the first pitch. I missed it. I missed two more, fouled one off, and hit one past Ross.

"You were one for five," he said.

Next, I put on my jasmine-scented wristband and sniffed it before each of Ross's five pitches. I clobbered all of them.

"That's incredible!" Ross exclaimed. "Those things really work."

"They helped me feel more comfortable at the plate," I explained.

"I could see that because you had a more natural swing than you did before," said Ross, adding that the jasmine scent is very relaxing. "I might use one of those wristbands myself. Then we could both make it to the majors."

"If," I said, "you don't mind playing for the Cubs."

"The Ride Stuff"

As a guy who is often compared to the back end of a horse, I had always wanted to see how the other half lives. I got a chance recently when I met Frank, the mane man at Greenlawn Equestrian Center on Long Island, where I had gone for a horseback riding lesson.

I was very impressed with Frank, not only because he is a retired police horse who used to work for the NYPD (if a cop show were filmed in his stall, it would be called "Law & Odor"), but because he stands 16.3 hands high (five-foot-seven at the withers, though he is more than six feet tall at his full height) and weighs about twelve-hundred pounds, roughly the size of New Jersey Governor Chris Christie.

At thirteen, Frank is too old by horse standards to be chasing bad guys, but he can still outrun the fastest human, even with a police partner—or, in my case, an eccentric equestrian—on his back.

According to a gallop poll conducted by trainer Hannie van Kretschmar, Frank didn't run, trot, or canter during my lesson, but he did saunter, stroll, and otherwise walk.

"Frank is a sweetheart," said Hannie, twenty-four, a proud graduate of the Lookout Mountain School of Horseshoeing in Gadsden, Alabama. "He's strong but gentle. And he has a good life here."

"You mean he leads a stable existence?" I asked.

"Definitely," said Hannie, adding that the same is true for all fifteen of Greenlawn's horses, who eat four times a day, have late-night snacks, and get their stalls cleaned twice a day.

"They also get pedicures," said Hannie, who keeps the horses' nails neatly trimmed so they can hoof it on out to give people rides.

"This is like a spa," I noted, "except it doesn't smell like one."

Hannie gave me a helmet (Frank didn't need one) and led us both outside, where I stood on a platform so I could climb aboard.

Sitting atop Frank was like being in an SUV (Saddled Utility Vehicle).

"Frank is a Thoroughbred quarter horse," Hannie told me.

"If he had the other three-quarters, he'd be as big as an elephant," I retorted. Frank snorted.

"Technically," Hannie said, "he's a dark bay Appendix gelding."

"Poor guy," I said.

"The procedure helps keep males calm," Hannie explained.

"I can just imagine," I said, wincing at the thought.

Initially, Hannie led Frank, with me in the saddle, around a covered ring. But after giving me instructions on how to handle the horse—tugging on the reins to steer him left or right, pulling back and using voice commands to put on the brakes, directing him around orange cones, standing in the stirrups and leaning forward in a two-point position—Hannie let me take control of Frank myself.

"You're doing an excellent job," she said as she walked alongside.

"Are you talking to me or Frank?" I asked.

"Both of you," Hannie replied.

It was clear that Frank and I had bonded. Yes, it's a guy thing (or, in his case, a former guy thing), but we hit it off beautifully.

When the half-hour lesson was over, I dismounted without breaking a leg, in which case I would have to be shot, and told Frank he was great. He shook his head.

"You're too modest," I said. Then I asked Hannie if I had the potential to be an equestrian in the next Olympics.

"Maybe," she answered.

I turned to Frank and said, "Want to go for it?"

Frank didn't say nay.

"Let's Get Physical"

Even though I was edged out by Hollywood hunk Bradley Cooper as People magazine's Sexiest Man Alive, I am proud to say that, for a guy with an AARP card, I still have a boyish figure. So I wasn't surprised when a personal trainer said that I have more fat in my head than I do on my body.

Del Davis, who also has a boyish figure, as well as an AARP card, made the calculation during my complimentary four-day membership at Eastern Athletic, a health club in Melville, New York.

Aside from adhering to a strict regimen of twelve-ounce curls, I hadn't worked out in decades. I may not be flabby, but I'm often winded just from getting up at night to go to the bathroom. Del had the unenviable task of whipping me back into shape without prompting People to name me Sexiest Man Deceased.

Del, who has been a personal trainer for twenty-five years, has amazing abs, bulging biceps, tremendous triceps, and other massive muscles. He also has youth on his side because he's ten days younger than I am.

"You're just a kid," I told him before my first workout. "No wonder you look so good."

"I am going to make you look good, too," said Del, who has won several bodybuilding championships in the United States and Canada, including the coveted title of Mr. Apollo.

"In college," I said, "I was known as Mr. Heineken."

For that reason alone, I should have keeled over thirty seconds after Del put me on a treadmill. Surprisingly, I survived the initial one-hour session, which included stints on a stretching machine and a pull-up machine. I also lifted weights.

"It's appropriate that I'm using dumbbells," I said, "because I am one."

"Not at all," Del replied. "I'm very impressed. If I didn't know you haven't exercised in years, I'd say you have been working out."

Fat chance. Which is why I was stunned at the beginning of my next session, a week later, to find out that I am a lean, mean geezer machine. Del took my height (six feet) and weight (one hundred and seventy pounds) and programmed the information into a small device that measures fat content. After I held it up in front of me, Del said that I have only nineteen percent fat.

"I have eighteen percent, so your fat percentage is great," said Del, adding that the average person has about twenty-five percent.

"Most of the fat must be in my head," I said.

"Definitely," Del replied.

The rest of the session was spent on an ab machine, a leg press, and a back machine. I didn't even break a sweat, though I was wearing sweatpants.

"Muscles have memory," said Del.

"Mine are too old to remember anything," I noted.

"Nonsense," he said. "Your muscles are bouncing back."

They were crying out in pain the following week, when Del stepped it up by making me step up on a machine called the versatile climber.

"Be like Spider-Man," he said.

"Spidey never needed CPR," I responded, huffing and puffing and almost blowing the gym down.

The rest of the session, which included a stint on a rowing machine ("I'm not going anywhere," I said) and a workout with a medicine ball ("I'm going to need medicine after this"), was equally intense.

"You did well," Del said afterward. "I didn't even have to call an ambulance."

The last of the four sessions was, by comparison, a breeze. I got back on the versatile climber, did pushups, pumped iron, and did bench dips. But the workout was more invigorating than tiring.

When it was all over, Del gave me an evaluation. On a scale of one to ten, with ten being the highest, I scored as follows: stamina, ten; agility, eight; strength, nine; fat percentage, ten; pushups, nine; dips, ten.

"And you don't even do anything," Del said. "I'm shocked. If you worked out regularly, you'd be off the charts. Overall, you're a perfect ten."

Take that, Bradley Cooper.

"The Smoke's on Me"

Everybody knows that cigar smoking can kill you, but very few people know why. Here's the reason: Whenever a man wants to smoke, which he can do almost nowhere these days but in his own home, his wife makes him go outside. And there, depending on the season, he either freezes to death or dies of sunstroke.

As the Bible says, ashes to ashes.

Still, I like a good cigar once in a while. And I have had none better than the one I smoked recently. That's because I rolled it myself.

I got a lesson in the fine art of cigar rolling from Julio Polanco, who runs a cigar company called, oddly enough, Polanco Cigars.

The first thing I found out when I went to his shop in Port Jefferson was that Julio and I have a lot in common. Like me, he has a wife and two grown daughters.

"Does your wife let you smoke in the house?" I asked.

"No," Julio said. "She makes me go outside."

"My wife doesn't let me smoke in the house, either," I said. "If I get a hankering for a cigar and the weather is lousy, I go in the garage."

"You're lucky you have a garage," Julio said. "I live in an apartment, so I have to park on the street."

"I guess you can't smoke in the car, either," I said.

"No," Julio replied, "but I solved the problem by opening a cigar shop. Now I smoke here."

"Has anyone ever wanted you to show him how to roll a cigar?" I asked.

"Yes," Julio said.

"How did he do?" I inquired.

"Not so good," Julio said. "But at least he didn't cut off any of his fingers. I bet you'll do better."

As I sat at a table behind the counter, Julio said I could choose one of three kinds of wrappers: Brazil, Sumatra, or Connecticut.

"I'm originally from Connecticut," I said. "Can I get frequent flier miles if I choose either Brazil or Sumatra?"

"I don't think so," Julio said.

"In that case," I replied, "I'll take Connecticut."

144

The tobacco used for Connecticut wrappers is mild, explained Julio, who is from the Dominican Republic, where his father, Pablo, founded the company.

"The filler for our cigars comes from the Dominican Republic and Nicaragua, which gives them a better taste," said Julio, who gave me a wrapper and said the veins should go on the inside.

"My veins are on the inside, too," I said as I laid the wrapper on the table and tried pathetically to wrap it, not too loose and not too tight, around the filler. My fingers fairly fumbled as Julio looked on in amusement.

"You have to put the wrapper at the right angle," he said as he showed me how it's done.

I got the hang of it, sort of, until it came time to use a brush to apply a naturally grown glue (made with tree powder and water) to the edge of the wrapper. I got more glue on my fingers than on the wrapper. Then I had to use a rounded knife to cut the excess wrapper and the tip of the cigar without, somehow, giving myself an extreme manicure.

"You did it!" exclaimed Julio, who added that it would take me a while (perhaps years) to become a master roller but that I wasn't as bad as that other customer.

I took my cigar home and, a couple of days later, on a beautiful afternoon, went outside for a sensational smoke.

Would Sue have let me smoke my very own creation inside? Close, but no cigar.

Chapter 16

*According to statistics that must have been influenced by
Elizabeth Taylor and Larry King, half of all marriages
end in divorce. As a happily married man, I prefer to look
at the bright side: The others end in death. When you're
an empty-nester, certain medical issues and end-of-life
business pitches make you think about your mortality.*

"Papa Had a Kidney Stone"

For fifteen years, I had taken great pains to forget a terrible episode in which I hit rock bottom. Then, after I became an empty nester, another terrible episode made me acutely aware that the great pains were back. And so was the rock.

In what I feared would become a series with more sequels than "Rocky," I had my second kidney stone.

The first—now known as Kidney Stone I, designated with a Roman numeral to distinguish it from the next one, Kidney Stone II—struck when Sue, the girls, and I lived in Stamford, where I received great care and got the stone as a keepsake.

The second episode started in Stamford, on a visit to my parents' house, and continued after Sue and I returned home to Long Island.

As a man who has been known to withstand a hangnail without flinching, I thought I could tough it out. But as the pain in my left side intensified to the point where it felt like I was trying to pass a bocce ball, I said to Sue, "I think we should go to the emergency room."

Sue drove me to John T. Mather Memorial Hospital in Port Jefferson, where two unsettling things happened: I noticed the word "memorial" on the sign outside the building and I was asked if I was on a "do not resuscitate" list.

Otherwise, I couldn't have been in better hands. A nurse named Ron showed his skill as a mixologist by making me a cocktail that eliminated not only the pain but most of my already limited cognitive functions.

I told Tom, the radiologic technologist who gave me a CAT scan, that we had three cats. "Will I need three scans?" I wondered.

"Just one," said Tom, adding, in answer to my next question, "No, we don't have a DOG scan."

A little later, Dr. Perry Shapiro announced I had a kidney stone.

"It's pretty big," he said, giving me a prescription that included Percocet. Because I was still a little groggy, I didn't quite understand the rest of it, but I thought he said I could get the meds from a couple named Flo and Max.

Dr. Shapiro also gave me a paper strainer in the hope that this, too, would pass. Then he referred me to an excellent urologist named Dr. Albert Kim.

The next day, after I had an X-ray, Sue drove me to Dr. Kim's office in—how appropriate is this?—Stony Brook. As I got out of the car, I noticed a small rock in the parking lot. I picked it up and put it in the strainer.

In the office, a medical assistant named Grace asked how I was feeling.

"I think I passed the stone," I told her.

"That's great," she said. "Let's see."

I showed her the rock in the strainer. Grace's eyes bugged out of her head. "Oh, my God!" she exclaimed. "It's huge."

"Actually," I admitted, "I found it in the parking lot."

Grace laughed. Dr. Kim, who also was vastly amused, had already seen the X-ray. "We'll have to blast," he said.

"With dynamite?" I inquired fearfully.

"The Percocet is making you even dopier than usual," Sue noted.

Dr. Kim, who assured me that he wouldn't need explosives, scheduled the procedure in two days at a place called the Kidney Stone Center in East Setauket. Meanwhile, I had to fill out so many forms that my hand hurt worse than my side.

On the day of the procedure, I was prepped by a very nice nurse named Gabrielle. Dr. Rick Melucci, the anesthesiologist, did everyone a favor by knocking me out. Dr. Kim then used shock waves on my kidney stone.

I wasn't shocked that I felt much better. In fact, that evening I had a speaking engagement, and aside from the fact that I was still a little lightheaded, which isn't significantly different from the way I am most of the time, I was a smash.

Unfortunately, on a follow-up visit, Dr. Kim saw on an X-ray that my kidney stone wasn't smashed. "It's been nicked a bit," he said, "but it's still in one piece."

So he booked me at Mather Hospital for a ureteroscopy, a surgical procedure taken from the Greek words "ureter" (an extremely sensitive area of the lower anatomy) and "oscopy" (invaded by a scope the length of a boa constrictor).

The intention was to blast to smithereens my kidney stone, which appeared to be composed of concrete and asphalt. Despite the persistent fear that I would wake up as the lead singer for the Vienna Boys' Choir, I was in a pretty jaunty mood as I sat in the pre-op unit with Sue, who was at my side to provide comfort, support, and, if necessary, information about my living will.

"Are you diabetic?" asked Janice, a nursing assistant.

"No," I replied. "I'm Italian."

Janice laughed.

"It gets worse," Sue promised.

Sure enough, when Janice asked if she could take my blood pressure on my left arm, I said, "Either arm is fine. I have it narrowed down to two. Good thing I'm not an octopus or we'd have to do this underwater."

"Is he always like this?" Janice asked Sue.

"Yes," Sue responded. "I just ignore him."

I helpfully pointed out that I hadn't even been given drugs.

"If I gave you Sodium Pentothal, you'd be gabbing up a storm," Janice said.

"Please," Sue begged, "not that."

"Do I have a pulse?" I asked Janice.

"Yes," she said. "It's sixty-four. And your oxygen level is one hundred percent."

"I never got a hundred on any test in school," I said.

"You just aced oxygen saturation," Janice replied.

"Too bad the oxygen isn't going to my brain," I noted.

Sue nodded.

Mary, a nurse, came in to continue the prep work.

"Turn toward me," she said.

"I'm taking a turn for the nurse," I told Sue.

Mary looked at Sue and said, "You're his daughter, right?" Sue chuckled. Mary smiled and said to me, "I'm giving it right back to you."

She was just what the doctor ordered: nice, funny, and very good at her job.

Then the doctor (or one of them) came in.

"I'm Dr. David Paul, your anesthesiologist," he said.

"What's up, doc?" I asked in my best Bugs Bunny voice.

"I'm going to knock you out," he said.

I thought Sue, Mary, and Janice would kiss him.

After a brief discussion about allergies ("I'm only allergic to myself," I said), the doctor left and Brian, a nurse anesthetist, came in.

"Do you have any questions?" he asked.

"Yes," I responded. "Will you be giving me domestic beer or an import?"

"You'll be getting craft beer," Brian said. "It's the best-quality brew." He should know because a friend of his owns a brewery. "By the way," Brian added reassuringly, "I won't be having any during the operation. I'll wait until tonight."

"Cheers!" I said as Brian left. Then Dr. Kim came in.

"Are you behaving?" he asked.

"Of course not," I replied.

"Good," he said with a smile. "See you in surgery."

The operation was a success. The next day, Louise called from the hospital to ask how I was feeling.

"Couldn't be better," I said. "It's been a rocky road, but the stone is gone."

That was verified by Dr. Kim on a follow-up visit. He looked at yet another X-ray (one of these days, I am going to start glowing in the dark) and said I was stone-free in my left kidney. "But," he added, "you have a large stone in your right kidney."

"What do you suggest?" I asked nervously.

"Let's leave it there and see what happens," he said. "I'll see you in six months. In the meantime, drink plenty of liquids."

"You mean beer?" I said hopefully.

"Water," Dr. Kim replied firmly. "Lots and lots of water."

Six months later, I sloshed into the office. Dr. Kim said everything looked fine in my left kidney but that the stone in my right kidney was still there and appeared to be getting larger.

"If it drops," he said ominously, "you're in trouble. I think we should try a shock-wave treatment."

"But it didn't work on my other kidney stone," I noted.

"That's because it was in the ureter," Dr. Kim explained. "This one is higher but is in the kidney itself, so there will be more of a direct hit."

A week later, I was back at the Kidney Stone Center. The familiar faces—Gabrielle the nurse and Dr. Paul the anesthesiologist among them—made me feel comfortable.

A week after that, Dr. Kim examined another X-ray and said, "Good news and bad news." "What's the good news?" I asked.

"We broke up the kidney stone," he replied.

"What's the bad news?"

"It's now in three pieces."

"What does that mean?"

"It means that all three pieces are still too big to pass. I think we should try again."

Once more, with feeling (or, rather, without it, because I was knocked out), Dr. Kim scored a knockout. He finally pulverized the stone, reducing it to pieces so small that they would pass through me like sands through an hourglass.

I don't have an hourglass figure, but speaking of time, I had waged a yearlong battle with kidney stones. At long last, thanks to the efforts of Dr. Kim and all the other wonderful people who took such good care of me, my long abdominal nightmare was over.

"Now," Sue said, "the only rocks you have are in your head."

"Taken Aback"

I threw my back out, but the garbageman wouldn't take it. I don't blame him. When it comes to sore backs, I bow to no man. And if I tried, I wouldn't be able to straighten up.

That's what happened when I bent over (and not even backward) in an effort to be useful around the house. I'd just had lunch and figured I would be a good guy and do the dishes. So I opened the cabinet under the sink to get some dishwashing liquid. As I reached for it, I felt something—possibly the insertion of a hot fireplace poker—in my lower back.

I tried to stand erect but remained at a forty-five-degree angle, which I know was correct because I had haunting flashbacks to my high school geometry class. When I finally stood up straight, my throat emitted a blast not unlike that of a foghorn, which was appropriate since I'm usually in a fog.

Thus began a stretch in which I couldn't stretch—or sit, or stand, or walk—without experiencing the kind of pain normally associated with childbirth or having the mortgage payment extracted from your checkbook without Novocain.

So I saw a chiropractor.

"You overstepped your kindness," said Dr. Gary DiBenedetto of North Shore Chiropractic in Port Jefferson Station. "This is what happens when you try to be useful around the house."

DiBenedetto should know: He once threw his back out trying to repair his car.

"I was wrestling with some rusted bolts," he recalled. "I got up and felt like my spine had been ripped out."

"I'm rusty myself," I said, "so I let a mechanic work on my car."

DiBenedetto also remembered the time he hurt his back by jumping off the top of a mountain.

"I went to Haiti with my son on a relief mission after the 2010 earthquake," he said. "We walked through the jungle with our volunteer group on something called the Waterfall Challenge and came to a rock ledge. It was a thirty-foot drop into a waterfall. My son, who was fifteen at the time, kept saying, 'Go, Dad, go!' So I jumped, but not straight. My butt hit the water. You don't realize how hard water is until you land on it. I blew out my back. Here's my professional advice: Never jump into a waterfall."

In his twenty-two years in practice, DiBenedetto has heard it all.

"One guy hesitated before telling me that he hurt his back when he was in an unusual position with his wife," he related. "I said, 'I don't need to know the details, but now you know what not to do next time.' I see some crazy stuff."

Bending over to get dishwashing liquid ranks right up there, said DiBenedetto, who put me on an adjustable table and gave me an exam.

"You have a ridge on your left side that's higher than the right, which makes one leg shorter than the other," he said. "That can put stress on your lower back."

"I think the only thing that works for back pain is beer," I said.

"Alcohol is a muscle relaxant, so you may be right," said DiBenedetto, adding that only about twenty percent of his patients have back problems. "Many people have neck pain," he said.

"I'm a pain in everyone's neck," I noted.

"I can see that," the good doctor said with a smile. "Nerves also give people trouble, so I guess you have a lot of nerve coming here."

Because my back felt better the day of my appointment, DiBenedetto didn't crack it. But he did give me a brief education in chiropractic medicine. I came away from my first visit to a chiropractor with great respect for the profession.

"If you get hurt doing the dishes again, I'll be here," DiBenedetto said.

"Thanks, doc," I replied. "It's good to know you've got my back."

"Too Cuticle for Words"

As a man with his finger on the pulse of America, which could get me into legal trouble, I am happy to report that I still have a pulse after surviving an infected finger.

The trouble was caused by a hangnail that developed into paronychia, a bacterial hand infection that can lead to banishment from nail salons or, in extreme cases, death.

I can just imagine the lead of my obituary: "Jerry Zezima, a longtime newspaper columnist and certified public nuisance, died yesterday of complications from a hangnail. He was fifty-eight."

Actually, I am old enough to know better. But I didn't, which is why I plucked the stupid thing instead of using a nail clipper or, even better, a Ginsu knife, which is advertised on the company's website as being able to "cut through a nail," as well as a tin can or a radiator hose, "and still slice a tomato paper thin."

Fortunately, I don't have a Ginsu knife or I might have amputated my finger. Which may have been necessary anyway because the infection, according to several trained medical professionals, was pretty severe.

The first one I saw was Julia Leydon, an occupational health nurse at work. When I walked into her office on a Friday morning, she immediately noticed my right index finger, possibly because it was so big and so red that if I had been standing on a street corner with my hand raised, cars might actually have stopped.

"That doesn't look good," she said ominously.

"It doesn't feel good," I replied. "If it gets any bigger, I could be a float in the Thanksgiving parade."

Julia, who is certified in case management, stated certifiably that my case needed immediate management. She took me downstairs and said she was going to make me a cocktail.

"I could use a drink," I said. "It might numb the pain."

"It's a little too early in the day for the kind of cocktail you have in mind," said Julia, who whipped up a concoction of hydrogen peroxide and warm water, into which she gently immersed my finger. "Soak for twenty minutes," she instructed. "Then repeat three or four times a day. After each soaking, put some Bacitracin on your finger and cover it with a Band-Aid."

Julia gave me a few packets of Bacitracin, which is an antibiotic ointment, and several Band-Aids.

"Are you right-handed?" she asked.

"I'm ambidextrous," I said. "I'm incompetent with both hands."

"If you notice red lines starting to go down your finger," Julia warned, "you should see a doctor."

By the next morning, my finger looked like it was about to be the cause of one of those Hollywood movie explosions in which a fireball erupts and blows a guy (in this case, me) across the street.

Since it was Saturday, and I couldn't see my doctor, I went to a clinic, where an attending physician winced when she saw my finger and suggested I continue to soak it.

"Add epsom salt to the water," she said, giving me a prescription for an antibiotic. "If your finger isn't better by Monday, come back and we'll lance it."

By Monday, my finger seemed almost as big as my head, except that my head is empty and my finger doesn't have a mustache. I went back to the clinic and another physician said he would relieve the pressure by draining the humongous digit. The stuff that came out could have clogged a drain, but I felt greatly relieved.

I continued to soak my finger and finished the antibiotics.

"It's looking much better," Julia the nurse said when I saw her for a follow-up visit. "Next time you get a hangnail, don't pull it out."

"At least it didn't kill me," I said. "Then I would have been a victim of the fickle finger of fate."

"You'll Die Laughing"

I am wanted—dead or alive. And it's not the cops who are looking for me, though they probably have good reason. The guy who wants me—in my present condition, if you can call this living, and then after I have gone to the hereafter—is a funeral director.

I became uncomfortably aware that my business was desired when I started getting brochures in the mail from Moloney Family Funeral Homes, Inc., which has half a dozen locations on Long Island, where I live (for the time being, anyway).

"We guarantee you will be satisfied," it said in one of the brochures.

My immediate reaction was: "How will I know I'm satisfied if I'm not here?"

To find out, I went to the Moloney funeral home in Port Jefferson Station and spoke with co-owner Peter Moloney, whose grandfather James Moloney founded the business in 1935.

"Have you been talking with my doctor?" I asked Peter. "If so, I want a second opinion."

"No," he said. "But we do market research. You must be on our mailing list because you're over fifty."

"Baby boomers are living longer these days," I noted, adding that I'm fifty-eight. "You may have to wait a long time to get business from me."

"That's OK," replied Peter, who's forty-seven. "But the older we get, the more we have these occurrences. I always kid my doctor friends. I say, 'I bury your mistakes.' One doctor didn't like that. His wife had to come between us. Sometimes people are too serious. You have to be able to laugh at yourself a little."

That goes for Peter, who is often the butt of jokes when he addresses senior groups. He told me, "I've been introduced by the president of the club, who will say, 'Guess who we have with us today. A funeral director!' And the members will go, 'Oh, come on!' I'll say, 'You really don't like me, do you?' And they'll say, 'No, we don't like you.' It goes with the territory. But we always end up having some laughs."

The laughs began when Peter and his seven siblings were young and lived above one of the funeral homes. Their father, Dan Moloney, who had taken over the business, would tell the kids not to make noise while a wake was going on.

"He'd tell us to stop running around," Peter remembered. "After calling hours, we'd go downstairs. My father would say, 'Who's touching the hands?' He was talking about the deceased. Of course, we would deny it."

When Dan Moloney died, in 2001, Peter recalled, "We had a Jesse James carriage drawn by two white horses and paraded him all over Ronkonkoma. He once told me, 'Spend as much as you can on my funeral. And get a third limo for all my girlfriends.' He was a character."

Peter, a chip off the old block, said he told his wife, "I want my funeral at four in the morning so I can inconvenience everybody one last time."

He doesn't think he'll have a horse-drawn carriage, but a customer could order one.

"We've had motorcycle funerals," Peter said. "We've also had slot machines at the funeral home at the request of people who liked to gamble. One guy who loved to buy ice cream for his grandchildren wanted an ice cream truck. We had it in the parking lot so everyone could have ice cream."

"Here's my wish," I said. "I'd like an open casket, but I want my feet showing so everybody could say how good I looked."

"OK," said Peter, who recalled the "cantankerous little old lady" who was insulted when she received a brochure in the mail. "I told her, 'If you use Moloney's, you'll make it to heaven a little faster.' She laughed like hell and made an appointment."

When I told Peter I plan to be buried in my hometown of Stamford, he said, "We'll ship you up there." But, he added, not in a horse-drawn carriage.

"You'd get a ticket on the Long Island Expressway," Peter said.

I smiled and replied, "Over my dead body."

Chapter 17

Life is a bit slower—and a lot quieter—after the kids move out, but that doesn't mean you have to sit home and do nothing all the time. Every once in a while, you get to have a little excitement, even if it only entails going shopping, taking a day trip, or going out for burgers and beer. And you find yourself asking the eternal empty-nester question: Are we having fun yet?

"Seals of Approval"

Unlike a lot of seals, who have managed to gain steady employment in circuses and aquariums, I have never tried to balance a beach ball on my nose. Considering the prominence of my proboscis, nobody could tell the difference.

But I once was a seal trainer for a day at an aquarium. I even have a framed certificate and a photo of me being kissed by a four-hundred-sixty-five-pound sea lion named Herbie.

I figured this valuable experience would come in handy when Sue and I went on a seal walk with our favorite naturalist, Dr. Artie Kopelman.

A couple of years ago, Kopelman led me, Sue, and about eighty other people on a whale watch off Montauk, New York. Everyone but Kopelman, the captain, and yours truly got violently ill. Sue was green for three days. Even the whales must have been sick because none showed up.

There was little chance of a repeat on the seal walk because we would be on terra firma, not the open ocean. (The ocean, by the way, is open until nine p.m. on Thursdays.)

Lacking seal blubber, which made me want to blubber when I realized how cold it was, I was bundled in four layers of clothing to ward off the thirty-degree temperature, twenty-mile-per-hour wind gusts and twenty-degree windchill, conditions that are positively balmy for seals. Then again, I'm positively balmy myself, so I was prepared to perambulate with a pack of pinniped pals.

So were forty or so fellow seal walkers who huddled in Cupsogue Beach County Park in Westhampton and were warmly welcomed, figuratively speaking, by Kopelman, a college professor and president of the Coastal Research and Education Society of Long Island.

Before we set out on our walk, Kopelman warned, "Never get in the water with a seal."

That's because—if you don't freeze to death first—seals will eat you. Or try to balance you on their noses.

Peg Hart is living (fortunately) proof. "I was bitten by an elephant seal," said Hart, a naturalist who specializes in birds (she was, after all, talking to a birdbrain) but also works with marine mammals.

"It happened in San Francisco," Hart recalled. "The seal had to be restrained so its blood could be drawn."

Instead, the seal drew Hart's blood. "It was a fluke," she said, rolling up her sleeve to reveal a long scar.

"Looks more like it was a tooth," I said.

Hart left her seal in San Francisco. Now she's back East and going on seal walks with Kopelman.

Curiously, seals don't like to walk, preferring to take mass transit by swimming together, which made the seal walk a misnomer.

The two dozen harbor seals we saw were about a hundred and fifty yards away, lounging on the beach but not, as far as I could see, reading romance novels.

I did get a better view of them when I looked through Kopelman's telescope. One of the bigger ones turned on its side and waved a flipper at me. I waved back.

"I can see some of my regulars," said Kopelman, noting that a few of the seals return to the beach every year from Canada, where they have summer homes. On the water, of course.

Despite the difficult conditions, it was a fascinating experience. Kopelman, who has been leading such groups for more than twenty years, had great insight not only about marine mammals but terrestrial ones, too.

"A couple of weeks ago, this kid showed up in shorts, with no gloves and no hat," Kopelman said. "He must have eaten dumb flakes for breakfast. Then there was the woman who asked, 'Do seals have bones?' And some people want to know where the bathroom is. I always say, 'It's at home.' Thanks to humans, these seal walks can be a real adventure."

"Hello Deli"

"From New York, the greatest city in the world, it's the 'Late Show With David Letterman.' With Paul Shaffer and the CBS Orchestra. And Dave's special guests, Sue and Jerry Zezima!"

Announcer Alan Kalter didn't actually say that last part in his introduction during a taping of "Late Show" at the Ed Sullivan Theater. But Sue and I were in the audience because Sue won a couple of tickets in a radio contest by correctly guessing Kalter's hair color: red.

We were required to be there several hours before the taping, so we had a lot of time to kill. Trying to find something to do in the city that never sleeps, we had lunch at the Hello Deli, which is around the corner from the theater.

"Hi!" said the smiling man behind the counter. "What would you like?"

It was none other than Rupert Jee, who owns the Hello Deli and is a celebrity in his own right for his many appearances on the show.

The hoagies were named after the program's regulars, so I ordered the top choice. "I'll have the Letterman," I said. Sue, who'd had a muffin for breakfast, didn't order anything.

As Elios, one of the deli's four employees, made my lunch, which consisted of ham, cheese, turkey, sweet peppers, mayonnaise, oil, and vinegar on a roll, I asked Rupert if Dave likes the hoagie that's named after him.

"He used to eat it, but not anymore," Rupert said.

"It's heart healthy," I replied, noting Dave's past cardiac troubles.

"Yeah," said Rupert, "if you take out the cheese and the mayo."

I don't have heart problems, so I carried the hoagie to one of the five tables crammed into the tiny deli's two hundred square feet, sat down with Sue, and munched away.

"Yum!" I said as Sue picked at my potato chips. "This is delicious."

"I'm glad you like it," said Rupert. "Since Dave doesn't eat his own hoagie now, maybe I'll rename it after you."

When I suggested he put a Rupert hoagie on the menu because he's a star, too, Rupert said, "Sometimes it gets so hectic in here, people don't know who I am. One time a couple came in and thought the guy at the griddle was me. They said, 'Hi, Rupert!' Then they took a picture and ran out. The griddle guy got credit for being me. People will come in and say, 'Is this Rupert's deli? Which one is Rupert?' That's how famous I am."

Still, business was pretty brisk, with customers cheerily greeting Rupert, a trim, youthful-looking baby boomer who appeared to be in excellent shape.

"I used to eat the profits," Rupert said. "I have Christmas videos shot from the back. When I first saw them, I said, 'Who is that massive guy?' It turned out to be me. That's the great thing about the food business: Even if things are bad, you eat anyway."

"How did you lose all that weight?" I asked.

Rupert replied, "Ping-Pong."

Just then, a disheveled man with a gray, scraggly beard came in, lugging a large black garbage bag containing his worldly possessions. He ordered a sandwich and left.

"He's a homeless former banker," Rupert explained. "He won't take free food, but he will take money."

"Rumor has it that he won't take chump change," said May Chin, Rupert's business partner. "He wants big bills."

"And he smokes good cigars," Rupert added.

Sue and I went back to the counter, where I paid $10.04 for my hoagie, a side order of chips, and a bottle of cream soda.

"Enjoy the show!" Rupert said.

We did. Alan was in fine voice; Paul and the band were sensational; Barbara Walters did a good job reading the Top Ten List; the real guests, Jerry Seinfeld and Tom Brokaw, were terrific; and Dave, as usual, was great.

Only one thing could have made the show better: If Rupert had come on and brought Dave a Letterman hoagie. Hold the mayo. No baloney.

"There's No Business Like Shoe Business"

If the shoe fits, wear it. Then wear the other one because otherwise you would have to hop around on one foot and you'd end up spraining an ankle. That's why I was reluctant to hop to it recently when Sue, a world-class bargain hunter, took me out to buy shoes.

"We're going to the Bass outlet," she told me.

"That's my favorite ale!" I exclaimed.

"We're not going drinking," Sue said.

"Then you mean we're going fishing?" I asked.

"We're going shoe shopping," she said.

If you were to make a list of my least favorite things to do, shoe shopping would rank right up there with spraining an ankle and making a list of my least favorite things to do.

My aversion to footwear goes back to when I was a teenager and worked in a clothing store. I liked almost every aspect of the job, especially putting goofy notes in shirt pockets and joking around with the tailors. But I hated waiting on customers who wanted to buy shoes. It didn't help that I could seldom find their size. And if I did, I'd forget to take out the paper balls that were stuffed inside the shoes.

I don't think I ever sold a pair. After much sole-searching, I decided to pursue a different career path.

To me, shoes are things you put on your feet to prevent frostbite in the winter and athlete's foot in the summer, although if I didn't wear them, it would be a boon to the gas mask industry.

Most of the time, I wear sneakers. And even they have become annoying to shop for because you have to decide whether you want walking shoes, running shoes, hiking shoes, practically everything except what sneakers are supposed to be: relaxing shoes.

Sue, on the other hand (or, rather, the other foot), loves shoes. She'll never rival Imelda Marcos, but she has a lot more than I do.

Currently, I have three pairs, including the black dress shoes I bought for Lauren's wedding. She would have killed me if I'd shown up wearing sneakers.

Sue's mission in taking me shoe shopping was to replace the clodhoppers that had served as my black casual pair for the past five or six years. She also wanted to return the nice brown pair she bought for me last year (but which I had never worn) because they were identical to the brown pair I had been wearing since I got the black clodhoppers.

I perused the store's brown shoes and saw a pair I liked. I looked at the price tag. It said: $140. I had the same reaction I'd have if I took a whiff of my own shoes: I almost fainted.

"They're on sale," Sue pointed out.

Indeed, the price had been slashed to $25. Same with the black casuals I liked, which had been priced at $110. I tried on both pairs, initially forgetting, of course, to take out the paper balls. The shoes fit like gloves.

"Maybe I should wear them on my hands," I said to Sue. She shook her head and led me to the checkout counter, where she not only returned my brown shoes but produced coupons that helped make this the deal of the century: two pairs of shoes, originally totaling $250, for $1.45.

That's right: one dollar and forty-five cents!

I kept waiting for the other shoe to drop. It didn't.

"Not a bad deal," Sue, Queen of the Bargain Hunters, said as we walked out.

"Now that," I replied, "is what I call getting a shopping excursion off on the right foot."

"Stepping Out With LeBron"

I had mighty big shoes to fill when I went to the Nike Factory Store for a pair of LeBron James sneakers.

I like to think that LeBron and I have something in common: He can dunk and I've reached the age where I am starting to dribble.

But there is no question that, because LeBron has made millions playing basketball and I had to take a vow of poverty when I went into journalism, he has more money than I do.

So I was hoping he would help me out financially if I decided to get a pair of his LeBron X shoes, which were retailing for about $300.

Unfortunately, the superstar wasn't in the store when Sue and I showed up on a busy Saturday. But I didn't need him because I was helped by a friendly and knowledgeable sales associate named Sattarock Blackwood.

"I'd like to try on a pair of the LeBron X shoes," I told Satty, as he is known to his friends and customers. My mistake, not surprising because I am an uncool geezer, was saying "X," as in the letter, not "X," as in the Roman numeral for ten.

Satty, a cool young person (he's XXI), politely ignored my gaffe and replied, "We don't have any. They sold out in one day."

As a man who can best be described as economically challenged, I couldn't understand how so many people could afford to shell out so much money for a product that doesn't include a roof and an attached garage.

"They're expensive," Satty acknowledged. "I designed twenty-eight styles of LeBron X's, but I couldn't afford to buy them."

"You designed the shoes?" I asked, flabbergasted.

"Actually," Satty said, "I went online to the Nike website. I mixed and matched colors and different elements like wings and Kevlar laces and carbon fiber soles for the LeBron X. You can do it, too."

"Can I design my own shoe?" I wondered.

"Sure," said Satty. "You'll have to come up with a symbol for yourself. LeBron has the crown, for King James."

"Maybe I'll use a Z," I said. "It could stand for my last name. Or zero, so my shoe could be the Jerry 0. That's how much it would be worth."

Since I could never see Nike putting its "Swoosh" logo on my sneakers, I asked Satty if I could try on a pair of LeBron 9 Elite Away shoes, which were going for $179.

"They look like ski boots," Sue said of the black size elevens.

"Or Frankenstein shoes," I said. "But they feel good."

"I think you look cool," Satty said.

"Hon," said Sue, "if they could help you play basketball like LeBron James, you could quit your day job."

Unfortunately, it was a Catch-XXII: I couldn't even afford the lesser-priced LeBron shoes that could have made me a multimillionaire basketball star, so I looked at other kinds, such as walking shoes, running shoes, and training shoes.

"You don't have lounging shoes, do you?" I asked.

"No," Satty answered. "I think those are called slippers."

I settled for a pair of white trainers, which were almost as comfortable as slippers. They didn't have wings or Kevlar laces or carbon fiber soles, and they didn't have anyone's symbol on the back, but they did come with a great price tag: $49.99.

"You got a good deal," Sue said.

"And you still look cool," Satty added.

"Thanks," I said as I strolled out. "If you happen to see LeBron, tell him he missed out on a terrific bargain."

"Killer on the Keys"

When it comes to pianists, only one—goodness gracious!—is a great ball of fire.

I refer to Jerry Lee Zezima.

With apologies to The Killer, Jerry Lee Lewis, who may indeed kill me if he ever finds out, I earned the name when I performed a flawless glissando in the last of the five piano lessons I took at Steinway & Sons in Melville, New York.

The crash course, "Learn to Play the EZ Way," was developed and taught by Vince Warren, a talented musician (he also plays guitar, dulcimer, and other stringed instruments) who works for Steinway.

As it said in a brochure for the class, "If your goal is to play Rachmaninoff's Piano Concerto No. 3 at Carnegie Hall, this class will not get you there. However, if you would like to play popular music, jazz standards, etc., with very little commitment on your part, then this class is for you. No musical experience necessary!"

I've always known that the best way to get to Carnegie Hall is, of course, by taxi. You also have to practice. And be able to spell "Rachmaninoff."

It was the part about very little commitment and no musical experience that sold me. After all, I had never played the piano, have never owned one, and couldn't even bang out "Chopsticks" or the Piano Concerto No. 3.

Still, I've always wanted to shoot the keys like Victor Borge, Chico Marx, and, above all, Jerry Lee Lewis. So I signed up because the piano, despite being difficult to play in a marching band, is my favorite instrument.

"It's mine, too," Vince said at the beginning of the first lesson. "And it's the most well-thought-out instrument. Notes you can learn to play quickly on the piano would take you months to learn on the trumpet."

That was good news to me and my two classmates, Marguerite and Joe, a very nice married couple who drew inspiration from the fact that Vince never took formal piano lessons as a kid. Because of his teaching method, we wouldn't have to take them as adults.

Like me, Joe had never played the piano, but he turned out to have a good ear for music. Or, as I told him, "two good ears." Marguerite had played before on an old family piano. I was at a disadvantage because I have a bad ear for music and I didn't have access to a piano to practice on.

"Don't worry," said Vince. "I'll have you playing in no time."

He wasn't kidding. By the end of the first lesson (and helped by key guides, or "cheaters," which line up with the piano keys), I was playing "Ode to Joy," which unfortunately went for naught because Joy wasn't in the class.

"Like you, Beethoven didn't have a piano," Vince told me. "There's hope."

I didn't think so because Vince said that the key to music is math, which was my worst subject in school, if you don't count all the others.

Amazingly, I got an A (the key of A) in Vince's class, which cost $89.95.

Using a songbook titled "Favorite Songs With 3 Chords," we also played "Amazing Grace" (she wasn't in the class, either) and "Londonderry Air" (which sounds like the backside of an Englishman but is actually "Danny Boy").

The third of the five weekly sessions was a one-on-one with Vince, who told me I was doing well despite not having a piano to practice on.

Marguerite, Joe, and I learned rhythmic values, rolled chords, and, in the final class, glissandos, which are finger glides down the keys from one pitch to another.

When I performed mine, Vince exulted, "Jerry Lee is in the house!"

I may not be another Killer, but there was a whole lotta shakin' goin' on.

"A Timeless Tale"

I was born more than three weeks past my due date and haven't been on time for anything since. I don't even wear a watch because I don't care what time it is.

So I was delighted to meet a woman who feels the same way. She works in a watch store.

"Before I got a job here about two years ago, I hadn't worn a watch since 1989," said Brenda, a sales professional at a Tourneau shop where I had gone with Sue, who needed a slight adjustment on her otherwise steady and stylish timepiece.

"I've had only one watch in my life," I told Brenda. "It was one of those digital things. You needed two hands to tell the time."

"And the hands weren't on the watch," she said helpfully.

"Right," I replied. "Anyway, our place was burglarized many years ago. The crooks made off with my wife's watch, but they left mine behind. It wasn't even good enough for thieves. I was so insulted that I haven't worn a watch since."

"How do you know what time it is?" Brenda asked.

"I ask my wife," I answered.

"I found myself having to ask people what time it was," Brenda said. "More often than not, they were wearing watches that didn't have the right time."

"So you were always late?" I inquired.

"Yes," said Brenda. "I was notorious for it. At family gatherings, my relatives would place bets to see what time I would arrive."

"My family says I'll be late to my own funeral," I said.

"What do you tell them?" Brenda wondered.

"I'm in no big hurry to get there," I said.

"Is this true?" Brenda asked Sue.

"Yes," Sue said. "He's always late."

"From the day I was born," I said, "I've been the late Jerry Zezima."

"I'm more punctual now," said Brenda. "It makes good sense to be on time when you work in a watch store."

Brenda's watch, which said 2:47 p.m., because that was the time, was like Sue's, a nice but not extravagant timepiece that looked good on her wrist. It was similar to the watch in the large photo on the wall. That one said 10:10.

"It's always ten after ten in a watch store," Brenda explained. "It's the same time in newspaper and magazine ads. It's where you are supposed to put your hands on the steering wheel when you drive."

"What happens in the spring and fall when the time changes?" I asked.

"You make a wrong turn," said Brenda.

"You know the old saying: Even a broken watch is right twice a day," I told Brenda, who gave me a candy watch.

"I give these to little kids when they come in with their parents," she said.

"It says five minutes to eight," I noted.

"It's not good at keeping time," Brenda said. "But at least it's edible. And it's free."

That's more than she could say for the other watches in the store, the most expensive of which were Rolexes.

"They start at $5,000," Brenda said. "It depends on how much bling you want. They're made of precious metals. You can get a platinum watch for just shy of $60,000."

"That's the cost of two cars," Sue said.

"True," said Brenda. "But you'd never keep a Rolex in the garage."

A good, reliable, more reasonably priced watch costs about $300, Brenda said, adding: "A watch is good for your self-esteem. You have the ease of knowing what time it is instead of having to ask."

I didn't buy a watch, but I told Brenda I'd think about it and come back.

"If you get one," she said, "you'll never be late again."

Sue looked at me and said, "It's about time."

"Confessions of a Class Clown"

If life begins at forty, I am seventeen years old, which was exactly my age when I graduated from high school forty years ago.

This was the belated math lesson I learned when Sue and I attended our fortieth high school reunion.

We are both proud members of the Stamford Catholic High School Class of 1971. I was the class clown, even though, still crazy after all these years, I have no class.

My goal in life was to be silly and irresponsible and actually get paid for it, which is why I became a humor columnist. My decision could be encapsulated in one word: algebra.

Here, as I dimly recall, which is how I recall most things these days, is the typical algebra problem:

The Smiths are leaving New York for Boston at nine a.m., averaging fifty-five miles per hour. The Joneses are leaving Boston for New York at ten a.m., averaging fifty miles per hour.

Question: At what point in the two-hundred-mile journey will they pass each other?

Answer: Who cares?

This was my attitude toward high school algebra, which explains why I got a D, which stood, of course, for Dumb.

I always did better in classes where I really didn't have to know the answers. I was especially good on essay tests because I could bluff my way through them. If high schools gave BS degrees, I would have graduated magna cum laude.

In an English class, each of us was assigned to write an essay on the same topic (I forget what it was) and get up in front of the class to read it. Nobody wanted to do this—except me. Everybody took it seriously—except me.

I wrote the silliest, stupidest, craziest, funniest stuff I could think of. When it was my turn, I got up in front of the class, read my essay, and got big laughs. I thought: Maybe I could do this for a living.

All the teachers at Catholic High were extremely supportive. Even though they were too kind to say so, they strongly implied that I was spectacularly unqualified to do anything else.

One teacher, a very smart, decent, and patient guy, wore an obvious toupee. I'd often go up to him and say, "What's on your mind?"

Yes, it was sophomoric. Then again, I had his class in sophomore year.

Another teacher, also a terrific guy, caught me playing floor hockey in home room. He told me to go home that night and write, one hundred times, on lined paper and in my best handwriting, "I will not play floor hockey in class," and bring the paper back to him the next morning.

"Very good, Mr. Zezima," the teacher said when he saw I had completed my punishment. "I hope you have learned your lesson." Then he gave the paper back to me.

Instead of throwing it out, I put it in my notebook. The following week, I was caught playing floor hockey again. The teacher once more assigned me to write, one hundred times, "I will not play floor hockey in class."

I went home that night and watched TV. The next morning, I handed the teacher my original paper. "Very good, Mr. Zezima," he said. "I hope you have learned your lesson."

I did, indeed. From this teacher, I learned creativity and ingenuity. In fact, I learned a lot at Catholic High and had a good time in the process.

The best thing that happened to me in high school was that I met Sue, who at the time was dating someone else. On the advice of my attorney, I can't say who or where he is, but he didn't show up at the reunion, which was a lot of fun.

Sue and I laughed, danced, and reminisced with old friends. And everyone looked great, especially Sue.

I did, however, resist the urge to play floor hockey. Maybe, if I can find my notebook, I'll do it at our fiftieth.

"Isn't It Romantic?"

When it comes to life in the fast lane, Sue and I are on the side of the road with a flat tire. If our lives were made into a sitcom or, God forbid, a reality show, the typical episode would show us struggling to stay awake for the eleven o'clock news.

"Sometimes," Sue once admitted, "it can get pretty boring."

That's why we decided to spice things up on a Saturday night and go out for burgers and beer at Billie's 1890 Saloon in Port Jefferson.

We drove a couple of miles into town and found a spot in a municipal lot, where I dutifully put seventy-five cents in the meter because—big spender that I am—I didn't want to get a ticket and ruin our enchanted evening.

We strolled into Billie's, made our way past the bar, and got a table in the back.

"How are you guys doing?" asked Mary Ann, our waitress, as she handed us menus.

"Fine, thank you," I replied with a broad smile. "My wife and I are on a hot date."

"You picked the right place," said Mary Ann, who took our drink order—two beers—and said she'd be right back.

I took Sue's hand from across the table.

"Isn't this romantic?" I asked.

"Very," she replied sweetly.

Mary Ann returned, took our dinner order—two burgers—and said she'd be right back again.

Sue and I gazed into each other's eyes. Then we talked about household projects, the need to put flea repellent on the cats, how the girls were doing and if, dear Lord, they'll ever come to get some of the stuff they still have in the garage, and other important issues that we never seem to have the time to talk about during the week.

"This is the only time we have to catch up," Sue said.

"Ketchup?" I replied, handing her the bottle on the table. "It's right here."

Mary Ann returned with our burgers, which were delicious. When Sue and I had finished, Mary Ann asked, "Would you like the check?"

"Not really," I replied. "But if you insist."

It came to $26.30. I left a seven-dollar tip.

Sue and I walked out of Billie's, ambled hand-in-hand down Main Street, turned left onto Mill Creek Road, and strolled through Chandler Square. We stopped at the Port Jeff Brewing Company for some free samples.

"What would you like?" asked Andrea, who was behind the bar in the tasting room.

Though Sue and I had already had one beer each, the samples were small: three of the brewery's latest offerings in two-ounce plastic cups. Besides, we planned to walk around quite a bit in the refreshing air before heading home.

We hung around for about twenty minutes and chatted with Andrea, who asked if we wanted to take home a growler.

"Maggie might get jealous of another dog," I told Sue.

"Come on, hon," she said with a sigh. "I'll buy you a cigar."

We walked across the narrow street and entered Polanco Cigars, where I had once rolled my own stogie.

"Hello!" said owner Julio Polanco, who had taped a copy of the column I wrote about my cigar-rolling adventure on the wall of the shop.

"What kind would you like, hon?" Sue asked.

I looked into the large glass case and chose a Toro, the kind I had rolled, a mild cigar with a Connecticut leaf wrapper. It was only $5.50. "I'll get you two," Sue said.

"You're too good to me," I told her.

"You paid for the burgers," Sue said.

"I spare no expense for you," I replied.

We chatted with Julio for a while, then walked back up Main Street and stopped at Red Mango, which sells frozen yogurt and smoothies.

"You can make your own," said Sue, who poured herself a cup of Honey Badger yogurt, which she sprinkled with graham cracker and chocolate chip toppings. "Would you like one?" she asked.

"No, thanks," I said. "I want to keep my boyish figure."

Sue, who has kept her girlish figure, took out a gift card that someone had given to her. "There's ten dollars on it," she said. The yogurt came to $5.01.

"Next time, it's on me," I promised. "Just make sure you give me the gift card."

We both smiled and walked slowly up the street as Sue ate her yogurt. When we got to the car, Sue said, "This has been a lot of fun."

"The kids would never be able to keep up with us," I said.

The drive back was quiet. When we got home, Sue kissed me and said, "Thank you for a wonderful evening."

"You're very welcome," I responded with another kiss. "We should do this more often."

Then we went upstairs, got undressed, climbed into bed, and—you guessed it—fell fast asleep.

For empty nesters, it doesn't get much more romantic than that.

Epilogue

I knew Lauren and Guillaume were in the driveway the second I heard the car doors shut and the locking system give off its distinctive *beep*. I also heard the tinkle of tags, so I knew Maggie was with them.

I just got home from work on a warm weekday evening to find that Sue had gone for a walk.

BANG BANG BANG!

It was Lauren, undaintily using her right fist to announce their arrival by pounding on the front door, an action necessitated by the fact that the doorbell, out of commission for years, still didn't work.

I rushed downstairs and opened the door.

"Hi!" Lauren chirped.

Maggie rushed in. Lauren unclipped the leash so the dynamic doggie could greet me by jumping up, pawing my shirt, and slobbering me with kisses. Guillaume, who didn't jump but did give me a hug, followed.

"Where's Mom?" Lauren asked.

"She's out for a walk," I answered. "She should be home in about ten minutes. To what do we owe this honor?"

"We just thought we'd stop by," Lauren said.

It was a little unusual because Lauren and Guillaume, who used to live in an apartment about five minutes down the road, had moved farther out east on Long Island and were now in a house more than half an hour away.

Still, it was great to have them close by. Katie and Dave, by contrast, had for years lived in Massachusetts before Katie got a fellowship to the University of Michigan. She and Dave lived in Ann Arbor for several months before continuing to heed Horace

Greeley's words to go west, young people. They settled in Los Angeles.

Fortunately, they weren't there for long before Katie got a job in New Jersey and Dave found work in New York City. They rented an apartment in Jersey a couple of hours from our house on the Island.

That meant both of our daughters would be as close to home as they had been since Katie graduated from college and moved—with my painful help—into that apartment in Boston.

I also was thrilled that I would get to see both Dave and Guillaume—my boys, my crew, the sons I never had.

Lauren and Guillaume sat down in the family room.

"Would you like anything?" I asked.

"Just a glass of water, please," said Guillaume, who usually doesn't have anything stronger than a sports drink.

"Would you like a glass of wine?" I asked Lauren, who does.

"No, thanks," she said. "I'll just have water."

It, too, was a little unusual, but I didn't think anything of it. We chatted for a bit until Sue came home.

After a minute or so of small talk, Lauren and Guillaume held hands as they faced Sue and me.

"We have something to tell you," Lauren said, beaming. "There's going to be an addition to the family."

I was stunned. "You're getting another dog?" I blurted.

Lauren rolled her eyes. She beamed again and announced, "I'm expecting a baby!"

I gasped. Sue shrieked. I jumped. Sue clapped. Then we both let out a whoop of joy, hugged and kissed Lauren, hugged and kissed Guillaume, hugged and kissed each other, and hugged and kissed Maggie, who was very excited to know she was going to be a big sister.

"Why don't you stay for dinner?" Sue said.

"OK," said Lauren, who informed me that I had a job: "You have to paint."

"I told Mom I'm retired from painting," I said. "She wants me to do the hallway."

"Not your house," Lauren said. "Our house. You have to paint the baby's room."

"I just came out of retirement," I declared. "I'll even paint your old room upstairs. You know, for when the baby comes over."

The evening was unforgettable. And it reinforced a beautiful lesson that Sue and I already knew: Even when the nest is empty, it's never that way for long.

Made in the USA
Middletown, DE
10 May 2017